# Donna Kooler's
# Seasons in Cross-Stitch

# Donna Kooler's
# Seasons in Cross-Stitch

**STERLING PUBLISHING CO., INC NEW YORK**
A STERLING/CHAPELLE BOOK

For Chapelle, Ltd.

Owner
Jo Packham

Editors
Ann Bear, Malissa Moody Boatwright

Staff
Marie Barber, Areta Bingham, Kass Burchett,
Rebecca Christensen, Holly Fuller, Marilyn Goff,
Shirley Heslop, Holly Hollingsworth, Shawn Hsu,
Susan Jorgensen, Leslie Liechty, Pauline Locke,
Ginger Mikkelsen, Barbara Milburn, Linda Orton,
Karmen Quinney, Rhonda Rainey, Leslie Ridenour,
Cindy Stoeckl

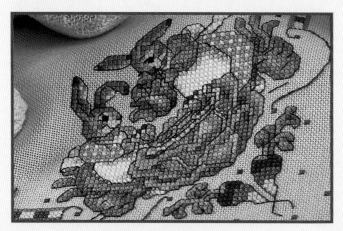

Library of Congress Cataloging-in-Publication Data

Kooler, Donna.
    Donna Kooler's seasons in cross-stitch.
        p.    cm.
    "A Sterling/Chapelle book."
    Includes index.
    ISBN 0-8069-9455-X
    1. Cross-stitch--Patterns.  2. Seasons in art.  I. Title.
TT778.C76K668  1998                           97-43004
746.44'3041--dc21                             CIP

10 9 8 7 6 5 4 3 2

Published by Sterling Publishing Company, Inc.
387 Park Avenue South, New York, N.Y. 10016
©1998 by Kooler Design Studio, Inc.
Distributed in Canada by Sterling Publishing
c/o Canadian Manda Group, One Atlantic Avenue,
Suite 105, Toronto, Ontario, Canada M6K 3E7
Distributed in Great Britain and Europe by Cassell PLC
Wellington House, 125 Strand, London WC2R OBB, England
Distributed in Australia by Capricorn Link (Australia) Pty Ltd.
P.O. Box 6651, Baulkham Hills, Business Centre, NSE 2153,
Australia
*Printed in Hong Kong*
All rights reserved

Sterling ISBN 0-8069-9455-X

For Kooler Design Studio, Inc.

President
Donna Kooler

Executive Vice President
Linda Gillum

Vice President
Priscilla Timm

Editors
Deanna Hall West, Priscilla Timm

Designers
Donna Kooler, Linda Gillum, Nancy Rossi,
Barbara Baatz, Jorja Hernandez, Sandy Orton,
Holly DeFount

Design Assistants
Sara Angle, Anita Forfang, Laurie Grant,
Virginia Hanley-Rivett, Marsha Hinkson,
Arlis Johnson, Lori Patton, Char Randolph,
Giana Shaw

Marketing Director
Loretta Heden

Photo Stylists
Donna Kooler, Deanna Hall West

Photographer
Dianne Woods, Berkeley, California

Framing
Frame City, Pleasant Hill, California

Cross-stitch PC Software by R. Scott Horton,
Hobbyware, Fishers, Indiana

*If you have any questions or comments or would like
information on specialty products featured in this book, please
contact: Chapelle, Ltd. • P.O. Box 9252 • Ogden, UT 84409
(801) 621-2777 • Fax (801) 621-2788*

Due to the limited amount of space available, we must print our
patterns at a reduced size in order to give our patrons the
maximum number of patterns possible in our publications. We
believe the quality and quantity of our patterns will compensate
for any inconvenience this may cause.

KOOLER
DESIGN
STUDIO
INC.

We had a great time in selecting these special designs for you. They represent the studio's marvelous team work and total involvement from the beginning design concept, to actual design, to finished project, and finally to photo styling and photography. We each had very different reasons for choosing these designs — a special holiday, a favored design style, or a treasured time of year. These are our favorites and we hope they will become yours as well. Enjoy!

*Donna Kooler*

*Presented within is an unsurpassed collection of seasonal cross-stitch designs from our award-winning needlework calendars. Whether your taste is traditional or contemporary, there is something here for you. Today the name of the Kooler Design Studio is synonymous with quality designs from Linda Gillum, Nancy Rossi, Barbara Baatz, Jorja Hernandez, Sandy Orton, Holly DeFount, Deanna Hall West, and Donna Kooler. These designs are in demand all over the world and are regularly featured in magazines, books, leaflets, and kits.*

*"There is no season such delight can bring, As summer, autumn, winter, and the spring."*

*— William Browne*

# Table of Contents

## Spring

### 8-35

## Summer

### 36-69

# Autumn

## 70-91

"I saw old Autumn in the misty morn stand shadowless like silence, listening to silence."

— Thomas Hood

# Winter

## 92-125

*"Winter's not forever, even snow melts."*

*— e.e. cummings*

# Spring

8

# Noah's Ark

•Designed by Linda Gillum

Stitched on antique white Aida 14, the finished design size is 8⅛" x 10⅛". The fabric was cut 14" x 16".

Stitch Count: 114w x 142h

| Sym | DMC | Description |
|-----|-----|-------------|
| • | blanc | White |
| н | 209 | Lavender - dk |
| ♥ | 300 | Mahogany - vy dk |
| ■ | 310 | Black |
| ╱ | 317 | Pewter Grey |
| ▮ | 333 | Periwinkle - dk |
| Z | 402 | Mahogany - lt |
| ▲ | 413 | Pewter Grey - dk |
| ✗ | 415 | Pearl Grey |
| ◖ | 603 | Cranberry - med lt |
| ╱ | 605 | Cranberry - vy lt |
| ◆◆ | 606 | Orange Red - bright |
| ✕ | 701 | Christmas Green - med |
| ▎ | 704 | Charteuse - bright |
| ∥ | 725 | Topaz - med |
| ◖ | 738 | Tan - vy lt |
| ɪ | 739 | Tan - ultra vy lt |
| ʟ | 740 | Tangerine - dk |
| ⌐ | 754 | Peach - lt |
| ▽ | 758 | Terra Cotta - lt |
| ○ | 762 | Pearl Grey - vy lt |
| ◆ | 796 | Royal Blue - dk |
| ⬤ | 798 | Delft Blue - dk |
| ★ | 815 | Garnet - med dk |
| = | 841 | Beige Brown - lt |
| ↑ | 842 | Beige Brown - vy lt |
| – | 3325 | Baby Blue - lt |
| ∨ | 3608 | Fuchsia - med |
| ✚ | 3776 | Mahogany - med lt |
| ⊕ | 3827 | Golden Brown - vy lt |
| m | 5282 | Gold Metallic |

## Backstitch: stitch in order listed
(1 strand except where noted)

310 - skunks' outlines; raccoon's mask, eye, nose, and ears; saying; Noah's eyes; giraffes' eyes and eyelashes; lion's eyes, eyelids, and nose; lioness' eye, eyelid, and nose; flamingoes' eyes and eyebrows; pelicans' eyes; pigs' eyes; bears' eyes and noses; rabbit's eyes; hippos' eyes and noses; sheep's eyes and noses

310 - cuff of sleeves (2 strands)

413 - dove's outline; olive branch; ark; mouse outline; flamingoes' outlines; hippos' outlines, mouth, and bridges of noses; greenery; ark's hill

413 - mouse's tail (2 strands)

317 - cloud; Noah's robe, beard, and mustache; sheep's outlines, mouths, and muzzles; pelicans' outlines; butterfly

300 - sun's outline; pigs' outlines; lion's outline; lioness' outline; rabbit's outline, nose, and muzzle; fish's outlines; raccoons' outline; giraffes' outlines; Noah's lips, nose, eyebrows, wrinkle lines, and hands; bears' outlines and eyebrows

102C (Kreinik's Vatican Gold cord) - criss-cross decoration over black portion of robe

## French Knot:

310 - mouse's eye; shunk's eyes; dove's eye; ellipsis dots; "i" in saying (1 strand)

## Straight Stitch:

725 - sun's rays (2 strands)

## Note:

1. For a commonly shared backstitch outline, choose the floss color of the object or animal which is in the foreground.

2. Sometimes a diagonal backstitch line will obscure a symbol beneath it. Choose a logical floss color closest to it.

## Model:

Cross-stitch: 3 strands
Backstitch: 1 strand except where noted

## Framed Piece Materials:

•10⅝" x 12⅜" frame.
•Mat set with 8⅝" x 10⅜" opening.

## Directions:

1. Insert design fabric into frame and mat set.

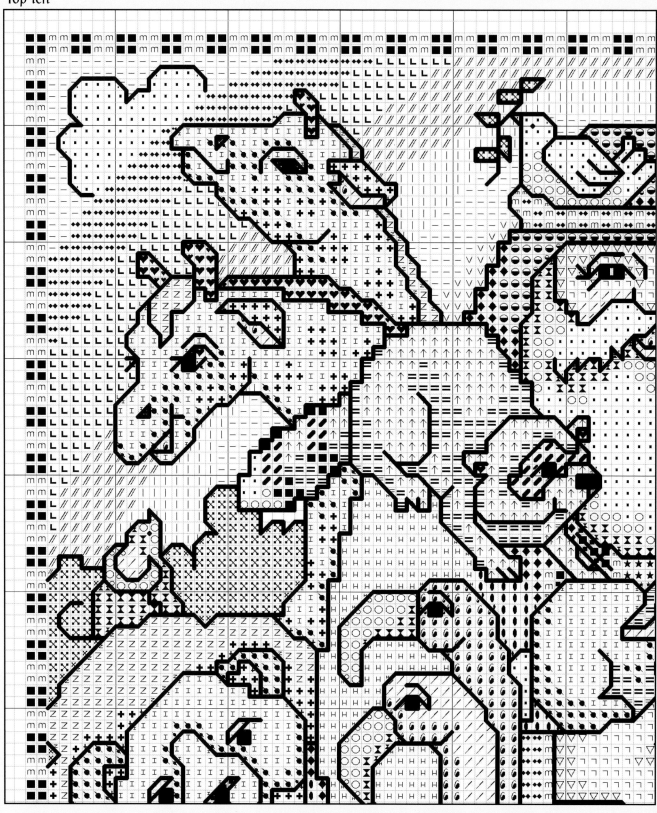

13

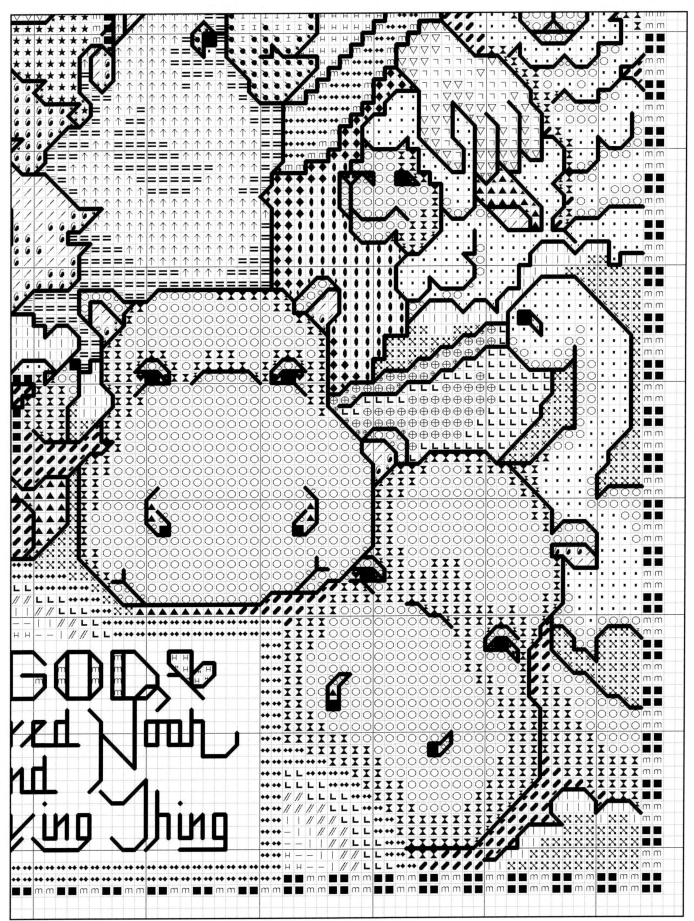

# Pansy Patch Bunny

•Designed by Nancy Rossi

Stitched on white Aida 14, the finished design size is 8½" x 5½". The fabric was cut 14" x 13".

Stitch Count: 113w x 77h

| Sym | DMC | Description |
|---|---|---|
| ▪ | blanc | White |
| Z | 209 | Lavender - dk |
| ■ | 310 | Black |
| ▲ | 312 | Navy Blue - lt |
| ♥ | 327 | Red Violet - dk |
| + | 341 | Periwinkle - lt |
| ∮ | 356 | Terra Cotta - med |
| / | 415 | Pearl Grey |
| ⇩ | 435 | Brown - vy lt |
| H | 436 | Tan |
| ∴ | 553 | Violet - med |
| ❶ | 640 | Beige Grey - dk |
| L | 676 | Old Gold - lt |
| ✓ | 726 | Topaz - lt |
| — | 739 | Tan - ultra vy lt |
| = | 741 | Tangerine - med |
| o | 746 | Off-White |
| ◖ | 760 | Salmon - med lt |
| ^ | 762 | Pearl Grey - vy lt |
| I | 772 | Leaf Green - lt (1 strand) |
| III | 772 | Leaf Green - lt |
| ⊥ | 945 | Pink Beige |
| ✕ | 966 | Baby Green - med |
| ⬤ | 989 | Forest Green - med |
| // | 3078 | Golden Yellow - vy lt |
| ◢ | 3346 | Hunter Green - med |
| ↑ | 3607 | Fuchsia - dk |
| ⊥ | 3608 | Fuchsia - med |
| ⤫ | 3753 | Antique Blue - ultra vy lt |
| ▷ | 3827 | Golden Brown - vy lt |

Backstitch: (1 strand except where noted)
 420 - bunny
 420 - bunny's eye (2 strands)
 435 - pansies with yellow or predominately yellow petals
 552 - butterfly body and antennae; pansies with blue, fuchsia, or purple petals
 987 - leaves and stems
 989 - tendrils (2 strands)

French Knot: (1 strand)
 blanc - dots on butterfly's upper wings

Note:
 1. Sometimes a diagonal backstitch line will obscure a symbol beneath it. Choose a logical floss color closest to it.

Model:
 Cross-stitch: 3 strands
 Backstitch: 1 strand except where noted

Framed Piece Materials:
 •10¾" x 9⅝" frame with 1"-wide paper liner with 8" x 6¾" opening.

Directions:
 1. Insert design fabric into frame and liner set.

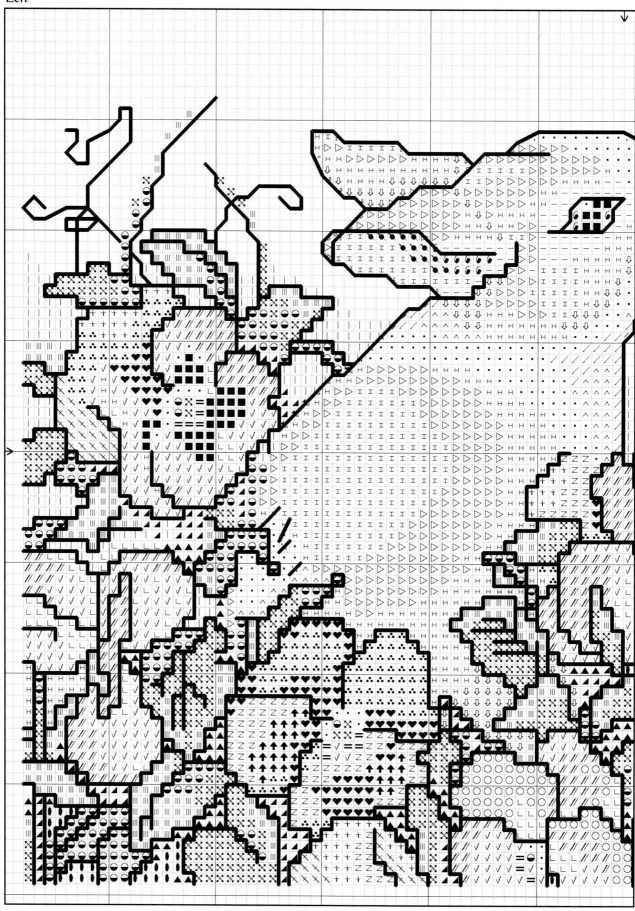

# Babes on a Branch

•Adapted from the Jean Beiermeister Collection

Stitched on ivory Jobelan 28-ct, stitched over two threads, the finished design size is 9" x 6¼". The fabric was cut 15" x 15".

Stitch Count: 126w x 88h

| Sym | DMC | Description |
|-----|------|-------------|
| – | ecru | Ecru |
| ɪ | 341 | Periwinkle - lt |
| ✖ | 352 | Coral - lt |
| = | 504 | Blue Green - lt |
| ■ | 632 | Rose Brown - vy dk |
| m | 676 | Old Gold - lt |
| ◖ | 729 | Old Gold - med |
| o | 745 | Yellow - vy lt |
| L | 754 | Peach - lt |
| ◀ | 758 | Terra Cotta - lt |
| ✎ | 760 | Salmon - med lt |
| x | 927 | Grey Blue - med |
| · | 951 | Pink Beige - lt |
| ♥ | 962 | Dusty Pink - med |
| 2 | 963 | Dusty Pink - vy lt |
| / | 3013 | Khaki Green - lt |
| ✚ | 3354 | Dusty Rose - lt |
| ▮ | 3712 | Salmon - med |
| ⌘ | 3753 | Antique Blue - ultra vy lt |
| ^ | 3756 | Baby Blue - ultra vy lt |
| ◆ | 3768 | Grey Blue - dk |
| ✕ | 3770 | Pink Beige - vy lt |
| ⬭ | 3772 | Rose Brown - med dk |
| ✦ | 3773 | Rose Brown - med lt |
| // | 3778 | Terra Cotta - med lt |
| ● | 3826 | Golden Brown - med dk |
| ★ | 3827 | Golden Brown - vy lt |

Blended Needle:

⊥      676 (2 strands) + 729 (1 strand)

&gt;      676 (2 strands) + 745 (1 strand)

Backstitch: (1 strand)

433 - branches; some flower and leaf stems (see photo)

3768 - butterfly's wings; blue and green dresses

3826 - yellow dress

3346 - midveins and outlines of leaves; remaining flower and leaf stems

3712 - flowers

3772 - bodies; eyes and eyebrows of all babes; hair

632 - butterfly's body and antennae

3778 - noses of all babes; upper lip of babe in yellow dress

815 - remaining lip outlines

French Knot: (2 strands)

3772 - flower stamens

632 - butterfly's antennae

Model:

Cross-stitch: 3 strands

Backstitch: 1 strand

Framed Piece Materials:

•10"-dia. wooden frame

Directions:

1. Insert design fabric into frame.

O Lord, how manifold
are Thy works!
In wisdom hast Thou
made them all:
The earth is full
of Thy riches. ~
—Psalms 104:24

# Psalms 104:24

•Designed by Nancy Rossi

Stitched on ivory Aida 14 (by Charles Craft), the finished design size is 7⅞" x 10". The fabric was cut 16" x 18".

Stitch Count: 111w x 140h

| Sym | DMC | Description |
|-----|-----|-------------|
| x | 209 | Lavender - dk |
| m | 341 | Periwinkle - lt |
| ✚ | 436 | Tan |
| ■ | 500 | Blue Green - vy dk |
| ▲ | 501 | Blue Green - dk |
| ○ | 504 | Blue Green - lt |
| ♥ | 552 | Violet - dk |
| ⌘ | 676 | Old Gold - lt |
| ^ | 727 | Topaz - vy lt |
| ▪ | 746 | Off-White |
| ✦ | 840 | Beige Brown - med |
| ◆ | 930 | Antique Blue - dk |
| • | 931 | Antique Blue - med |
| > | 3053 | Grey Green - lt |
| ⊐ | 3348 | Hunter Green - lt |
| ★ | 3816 | Celadon Green - med |
| ✓ | 3817 | Celadon Green - lt |
| ⊝ | 3826 | Golden Brown - med dk |

Half Cross-stitch: (1 strand)

| – | 3747 | Periwinkle - vy lt |
|---|------|--------------------|

Backstitch: (1 strand)
  3816 - leaves stitched in 504 green
  501 - all other leaves
  552 - dk violet flowers
  801 - branches
  3051 - lettering
  3826 - frame border; roses; stems

French Knot: (1 strand)
  3051 - lettering

Model:
  Cross-stitch: 3 strands, except where noted
  Backstitch: 1 strand

Framed Piece Materials:
  •11⅝" x 13¾" frame (⅝" wide) with 1¼"-wide liner

Directions:
1. Insert design fabric into frame and liner set.

*When I consider Your heavens, the work of Your fingers, the Moon and the stars, which You have ordained, what is man that You are mindful of him?*

*– Psalms 8:3*

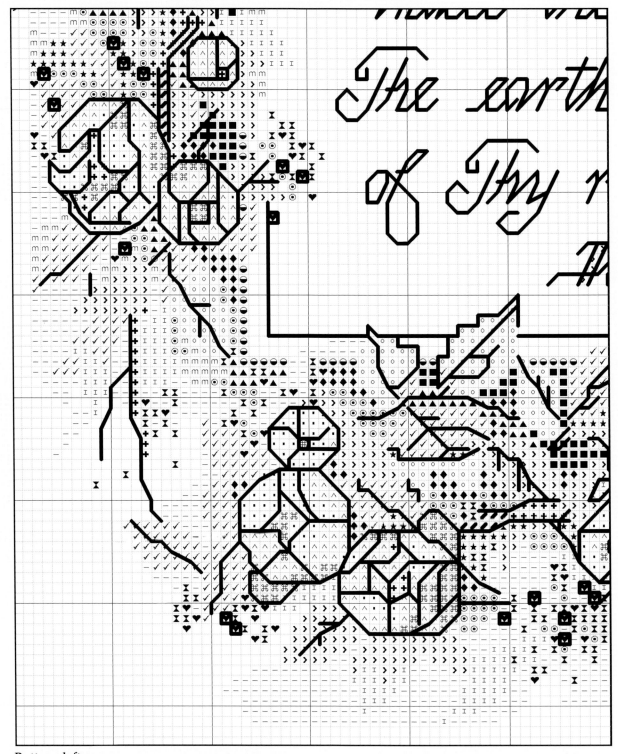

Bottom left

Bottom right

# Iris Portrait

•Designed by Jorja Hernandez

Stitched on cream Cashel linen, 28-ct, stitched over two threads, the finished design size is 9" x 9¼". The fabric was cut 16" x 16".

Stitch Count: 126w x 129h

| Sym | DMC | Description |
|---|---|---|
| ▪ | blanc | White |
| ▲ | 208 | Lavender - vy dk |
| ✓ | 209 | Lavender - dk |
| ✎ | 327 | Red Violet - dk |
| ⊖ | 420 | Hazelnut Brown - dk |
| ട | 422 | Hazelnut Brown - lt |
| ■ | 550 | Violet - vy dk |
| △ | 605 | Cranberry - vy lt |
| ◆ | 721 | Rust - med lt |
| Z | 727 | Topaz - vy lt |
| ∘ | 772 | Leaf Green - lt |
| ♥ | 791 | Cornflower Blue - vy dk |
| • | 792 | Cornflower Blue - dk |
| H | 793 | Cornflower Blue - med |
| L | 819 | Baby Pink - vy lt |
| ◥ | 972 | Pumpkin - vy lt |
| ▮ | 3041 | Antique Violet - med |
| ★ | 3346 | Hunter Green - med |
| ⊥ | 3347 | Hunter Green - med lt |
| ⋈ | 3348 | Hunter Green - lt |
| ✖ | 3607 | Fuchsia - dk |
| ⌘ | 3608 | Fuchsia - med |
| m | 3609 | Fuchsia - lt |
| ∕ | 3689 | Mauve - lt |

Backstitch: (1 strand)
  208 - lt-colored iris blossom
  327 - med-colored iris blossom
  550 - dk-colored iris blossom; buds
  3345 - leaves
  801 - everything else

Model:
  Cross-stitch: 3 strands
  Backstitch: 1 strand

Flanged-edge Pillow Materials:
  •15" x 15" cream Cashel linen (backing)
  •½ yd green marbled fabric (under pillow)
  •½ yd polyester clothing fleece
  •Ecru sewing thread
  •Polyester fiberfill

Directions:
  •Use ½" seam allowance.
  1. With design centered, trim design fabric to 15" square. Cut 15" square of fleece and baste to back of design fabric.
  2. With right sides facing, sew design unit to remaining linen square, leaving a 4" opening on one side. Turn design unit right sides out and press. Slip-stitch opening closed.
  3. Cut green fabric into two 17½" squares. Cut 17½" square of fleece and baste to back of one of green squares. With right sides facing, sew green squares together, leaving a 4" opening on one side. Turn right sides out, press, and slip-stitch opening closed.
  4. Center and baste design unit over right side of green square unit. Sew units together, 1⅝" from edge of design unit, leaving a 4" opening for stuffing.
  5. Stuff pillow with fiberfill, taking care to fill the corners and machine-stitch opening closed.

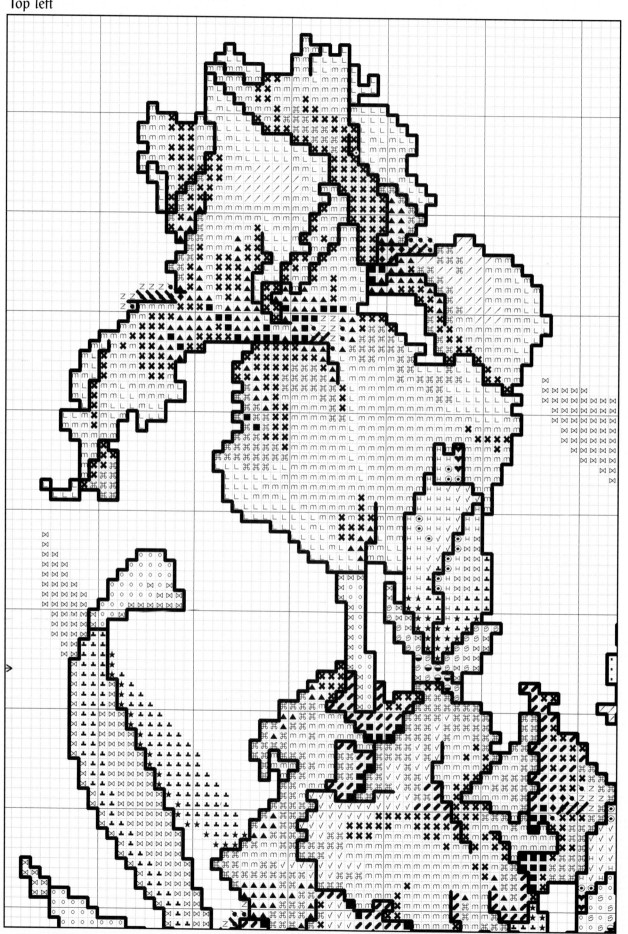

33

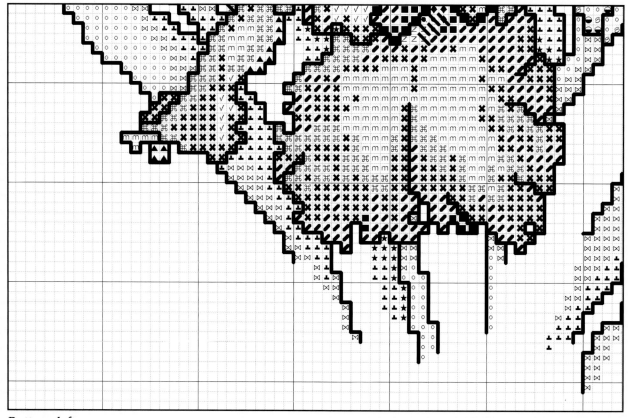

Bottom left

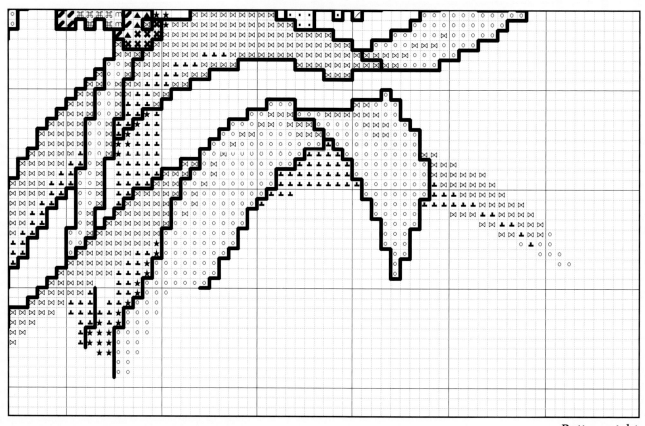

Bottom right

"In the garden after a rainfall, you can faintly, yes, hear the breaking of the new blooms."

– Truman Capote

# Sewing Sampler

•Designed by Holly DeFount

Stitched on black Aida 14, the finished design size is 8¾" x 6". The fabric was cut 15" x 12".

Stitch Count: 123w x 84h

| Sym | DMC | Description |
|-----|-----|-------------|
| ▪ | blanc | White |
| o | 209 | Lavender - dk |
| Z | 211 | Lavender - lt |
| ⊕ | 318 | Steel Grey - lt |
| ↓ | 327 | Red Violet - dk |
| ✕ | 350 | Coral - med dk |
| ■ | 413 | Pewter Grey - dk |
| ♥ | 433 | Brown - med |
| 6 | 435 | Brown - vy lt |
| L | 437 | Tan - lt |
| ● | 600 | Cranberry - vy dk |
| ↑ | 603 | Cranberry - med lt |
| = | 605 | Cranberry - vy lt |
| ✕ | 703 | Chartreuse |
| ^ | 739 | Tan - ultra vy lt |
| ✚ | 742 | Tangerine - lt |
| ▽ | 744 | Yellow - lt |
| / | 762 | Pearl Grey - vy lt |
| ◆ | 796 | Royal Blue - dk |
| m | 798 | Delft Blue - dk |
| – | 809 | Delft Blue - med lt |
| ▲ | 817 | Coral Red - vy dk |
| ❙ | 904 | Parrot Green - vy dk |
| ★ | 958 | Aqua - dk |
| v | 964 | Aqua - lt |
| ◢ | 976 | Golden Brown - med |
| I | 3823 | Yellow - ultra vy lt |

Backstitch: (1 strand except where noted)
  904 - leaves on tomato pincushion
  904 - tendrils on tape measure holder (2 strands)
  814 - tomato pincushion; floss (2 strands)
  814 - rose on tape measure holder; button card
  796 - blue portions of darner (2 strands)
  796 - blue portion of tatting shuttle and spool; buttons
  413 - thimble; label on floss skein; scissors; button card outline; outline of thread area on spool (2 strands)
  413 - hole on spool
  433 - darner handle; spool outline; needle holder; tatting shuttle outline; tape measure's handle (2 strands)
  3826 - tape measure's outline and inch marks
  318 - pin heads*

French Knot: (1 strand)
  413 - thimble depressions

Straight Stitch: (2 strands except where noted)
  blanc - button tacks (6 strands)
  318 - pin and needle shanks (2 strands)*

Lazy Daisy: (2 strands)
  318 - needle heads*

*Real pins and needles can be substituted

Note:
  1. Sometimes a diagonal backstitch line will obscure a symbol beneath it. Choose a logical floss color closest to it.

Model:
  Cross-stitch: 3 strands
  Backstitch: 1 strand except where noted

Sewing Basket Materials:
  •Oval sewing box
  •Two 8" x 10" pieces high-loft polyester batting
  •White fabric glue

Directions:
  1. Glue two layers of batting to mounting board (included with sewing box). Trim batting.
  2. Following manufacturer's instructions, attach design fabric to mounting board unit.
  3. Glue design unit into sewing box lid.

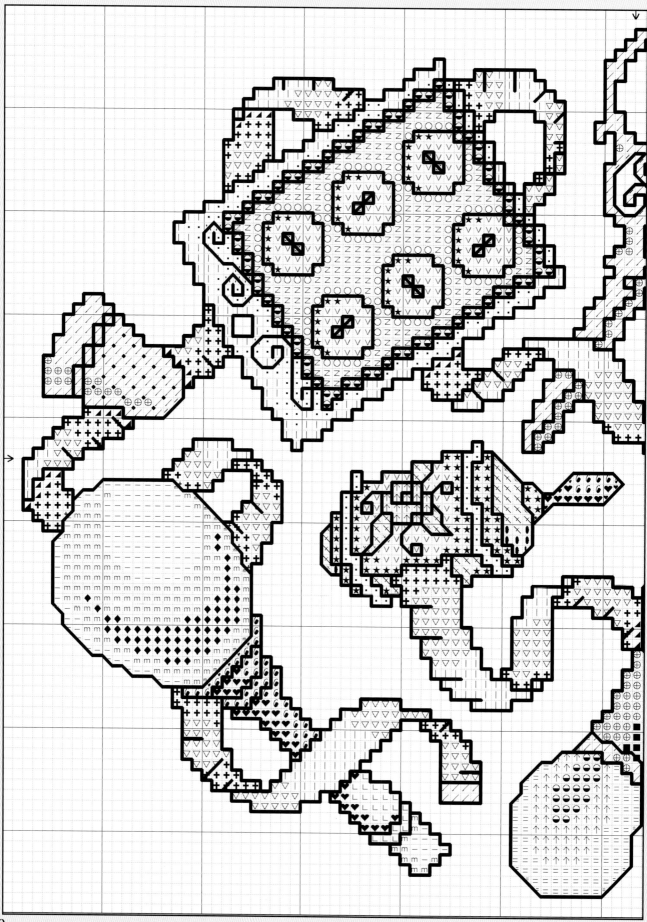

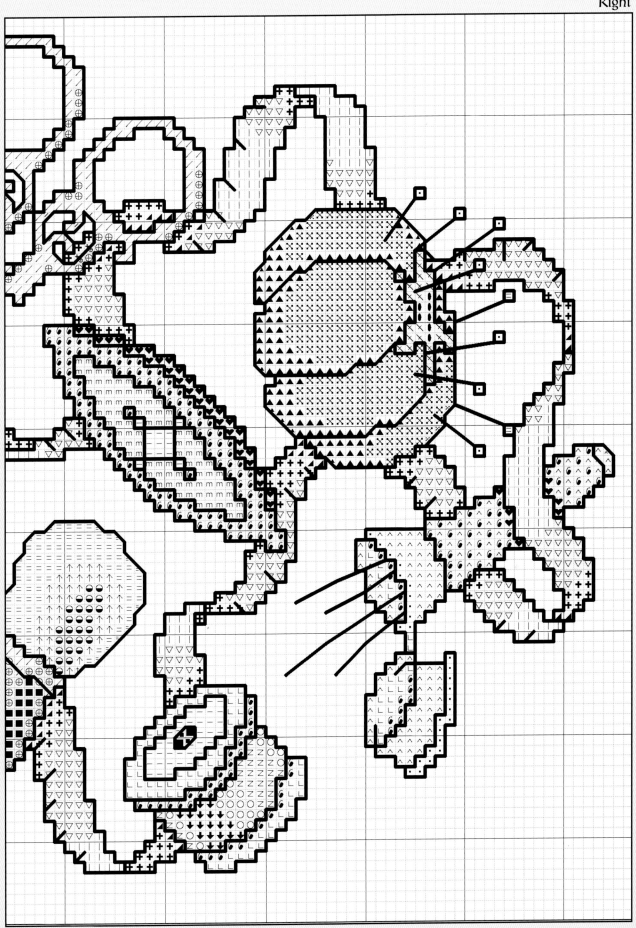

# Par Excellence

•Designed by Nancy Rossi

Stitched on white Aida 14, the finished design size is 8⅛" x 10¼". The fabric was cut 17" x 19".

Stitch Count: 114w x 144h

| Sym | DMC | Description |
|---|---|---|
| . | blanc | White |
| ○ | 209 | Lavender - dk |
| ■ | 310 | Black |
| ♥ | 333 | Periwinkle - dk |
| ⊥ | 340 | Periwinkle - med |
| ɪ | 452 | Shell Grey - med |
| ◆ | 500 | Blue Green - vy dk |
| L | 502 | Blue Green - med dk |
| // | 503 | Blue Green - med |
| ▲ | 552 | Violet - dk |
| ⊕ | 561 | Malachite - dk |
| = | 645 | Beaver Grey - dk |
| ✍ | 676 | Old Gold -lt |
| I | 677 | Old Gold - vy lt |
| ^ | 772 | Leaf Green - lt |
| _ | 822 | Beige Grey - lt |
| ↑ | 930 | Antique Blue - dk |
| ▷ | 931 | Antique Blue - med |
| ) | 932 | Antique Blue - lt |
| ★ | 988 | Forest Green - med dk |
| ● | 3012 | Khaki Green - med |
| ▽ | 3053 | Grey Green - lt |
| ↑ | 3064 | Pink Beige - dk |
| ❘ | 3607 | Fuchsia - dk |
| m | 3609 | Fuchsia - lt |
| 2 | 3689 | Mauve - lt |
| × | 3747 | Periwinkle - vy lt |
| 6 | 3772 | Rose Brown - med dk |
| ◢ | 3790 | Beige grey - vy dk |
| ✦ | 3799 | Charcoal - dk |

Blended Needle:

| ⇐ | 472 (2 strands) + 907 (1 strand) |
|---|---|
| | Chartreuse blend |
| ✕ | 907 (2 strands) + 704 (1 strands) |
| | Chartreuse blend |

Backstitch: (1 strand except where noted)
   645 - bridge; flagpole; golfers (2 strands)
   333 - blue-purple flowers
   340 - white flower
   552 - pink-magenta flowers
   500 - leaves

Couched Straight Stitch: (2 strands)
   645 - trees

Note:
   1. Sometimes a diagonal backstitch line will obscure a symbol beneath it. Choose a logical floss color closest to it.

Model:
   Cross-stitch: 3 strands
   Backstitch: 1 strand except where noted

Framed Piece Materials:
   •12⅛" x 14⅛" frame
   •Fabric covered mat with 8⅜" x 10⅜" opening

Directions:
   1. Insert design fabric into frame and mat set.

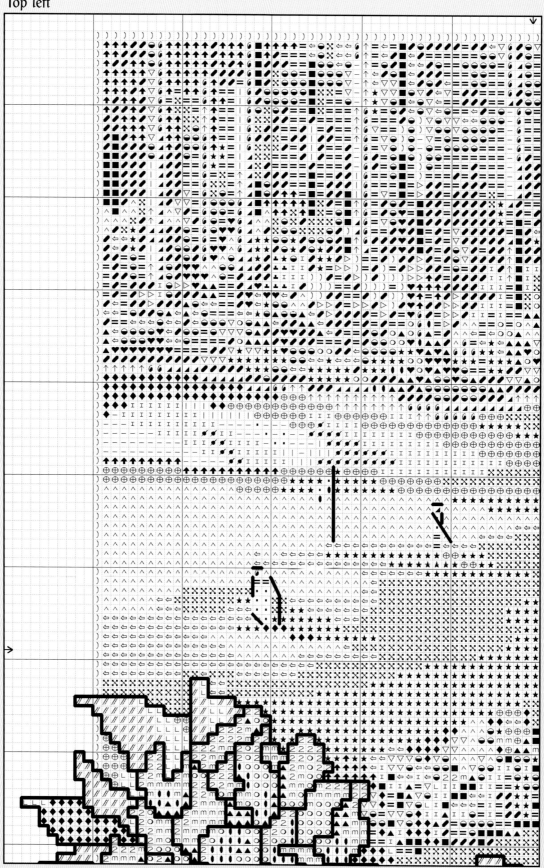

Top right

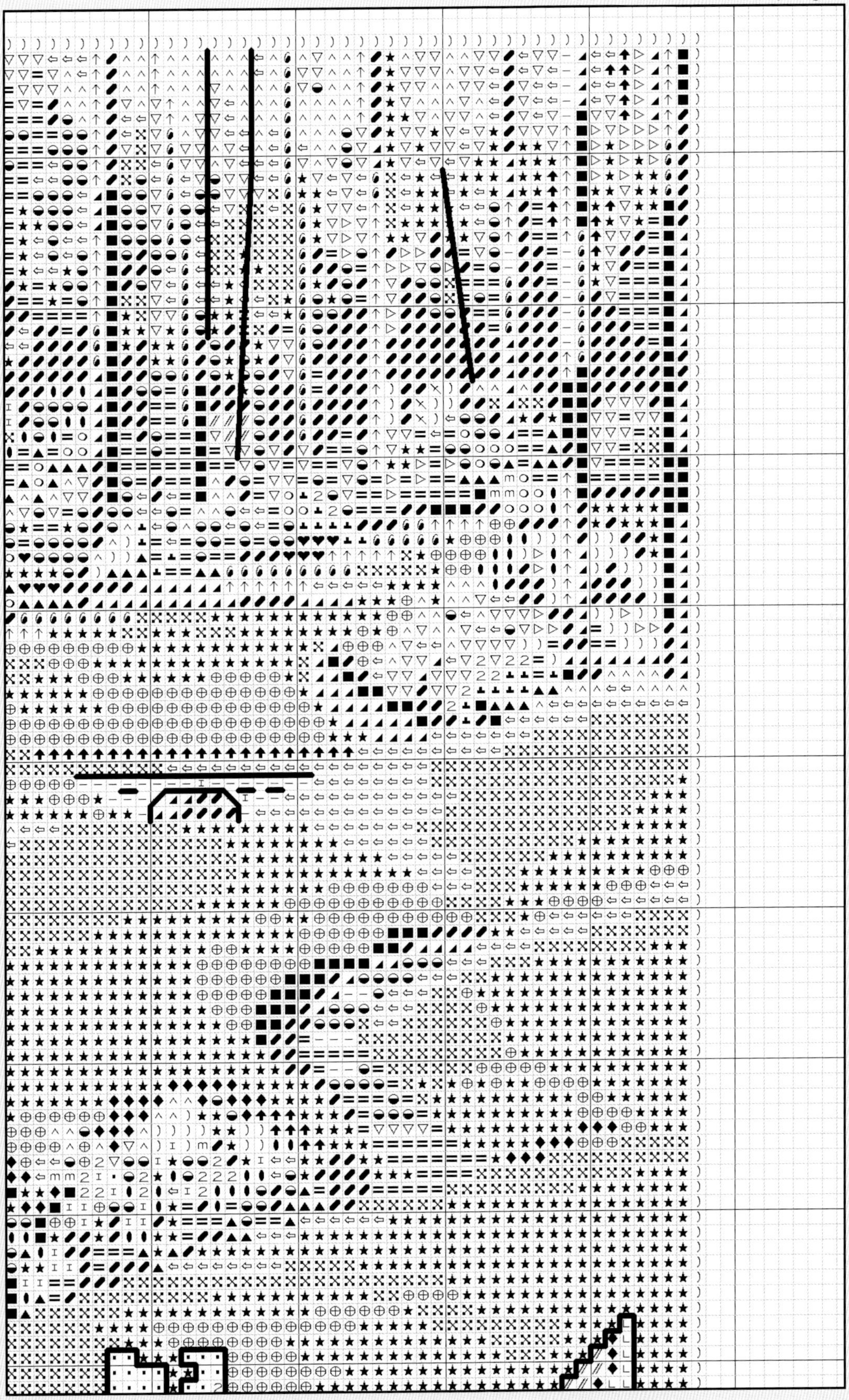

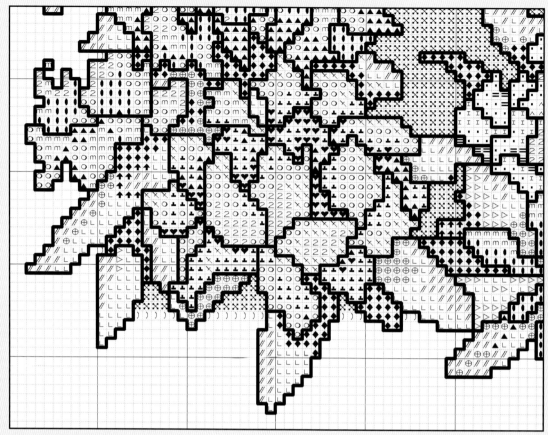

Bottom left

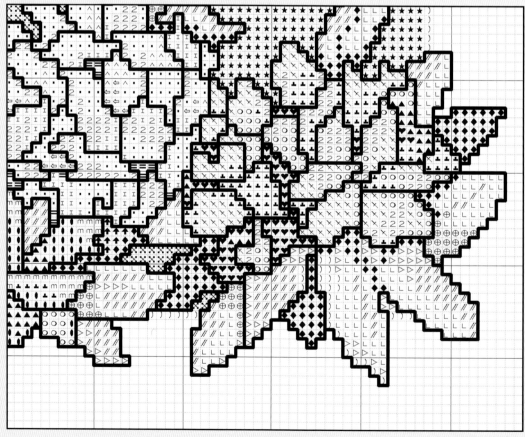

Bottom right

# Little Miss Sunshine

•Designed by Barbara Baatz

Stitched on white Aida 14, the finished design size is 6⅛" x 8⅜". The fabric was cut 13" x 14".

Stitch Count: 85w x 117h

| Sym | DMC | Description |
|---|---|---|
| ▪ | blanc | White |
| ■ | 310 | Black |
| ▲ | 312 | Navy Blue - lt |
| ♥ | 321 | Christmas Red |
| Z | 334 | Baby Blue - med dk |
| ❚ | 400 | Mahogany - dk |
| = | 472 | Avocado Green - vy lt |
| ◆ | 561 | Malachite - dk |
| ◆◆ | 562 | Malachite - med |
| ⁄⁄ | 722 | Rust - lt |
| I | 742 | Tangerine - lt |
| ° | 744 | Yellow - lt |
| ⁄ | 818 | Baby Pink |
| x | 840 | Beige Brown - med |
| ╳ | 892 | Carnation - med |
| I | 951 | Pink Beige - lt |
| m | 989 | Forest Green - med |
| ∕ | 3021 | Brown Grey - vy dk |
| − | 3033 | Mocha Brown - vy lt |
| ^ | 3325 | Baby Blue - lt |
| △ | 3708 | Strawberry - lt |
| × | 3776 | Mahogany - med lt |
| v | 3782 | Mocha Brown - lt |
| L | 3827 | Golden Brown - vy lt |

Backstitch: (1 strand except where noted)

561 - sunflower's stem and leaves; leaves on hat; green portion of apron; leaf on ground

321 - shoes; birdhouse roof; rose on hat; rose portion of apron

310 - crows' bodies, legs, and feet; kitten's muzzle and nose; doll's eyes and eyelashes*; bees' bodies, wings, and antennae; lower portion of birdhouse

840 - apron ruffle; pantaloons

3021 - lettering (2 strands)

3021 - kitten

312 - hat; skirt; blouse

3776 - mouth; nose; eyebrows (2 strands)

3776 - everything else

French Knot: (1 strand)

310 - kitten's eyes
*Make eyelashes one-half square long

Note:

1. Sometimes a diagonal backstitch line will obscure a symbol beneath it. Choose a logical floss color closest to it.

Model:

Cross-stitch: 3 strands

Backstitch: 1 strand except where noted

Pillow Materials:

•2½ yds of 3"-wide white flat trim
•1¼ yds of ¾₆"-dia cotton cording
•½ yd orange and white plaid fabric
•½ yd orange and white checkered fabric
•11" x 13" lightweight polyester fleece
•White sewing thread
•White pearl cotton thread (size 8)
•Polyester fiberfill

## Directions:

•Use ½" seam allowance.

1. Trim design, allowing 2" on sides and 1½" on top and bottom beyond the stitched design. Using design fabric as a pattern, cut one each of fleece and checkered fabric (backing).

2. Baste fleece to back of design fabric.

3. Cut and piece remaining checkered fabric to make a 2" x 42" bias strip. Using cording and strip, make piping. Trim piping allowance to ½". Matching raw edges, sew piping to right side of design unit, rounding corners and overlapping raw ends at bottom of design.

4. For ruffle, cut and piece plaid fabric to make a 7" x 81" strip. With right sides together, sew short sides. Press seam open. Fold in half lengthwise and press. Cut trim to 81" and, with right sides together, sew short sides and press seam open. Matching raw edges and, with right sides facing up, pin trim to strip. With a medium-length stitch, zigzag over pearl cotton ⅜" from raw edges of ruffle unit. Pull pearl cotton to gather ruffle to approximately 40".

5. With right sides together, pin ruffle to design unit. Arrange gathers evenly except at corners where more gathers are needed to prevent ruffle from cupping in. Sew ruffle and design unit together.

6. With right sides facing, sew design unit and backing together, leaving a 3" opening at the bottom. Clip corners and turn.

7. Stuff pillow with fiberfill, taking care to fill the corners and hand-sew opening closed.

*"You shall wander
hand in hand
with love
in summer's wonderland."*

*– Alfred Noyes*

Top left

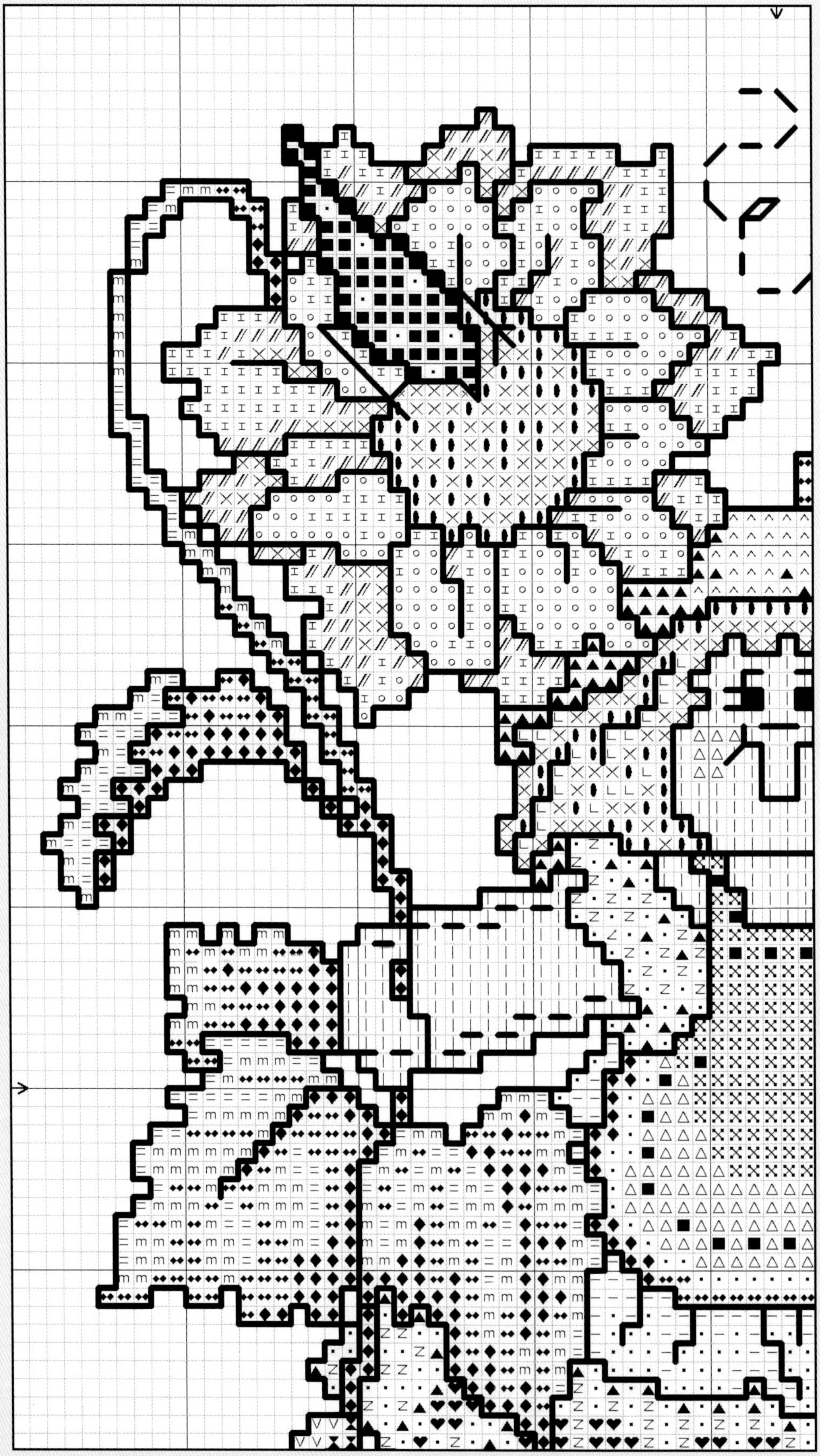

Top right

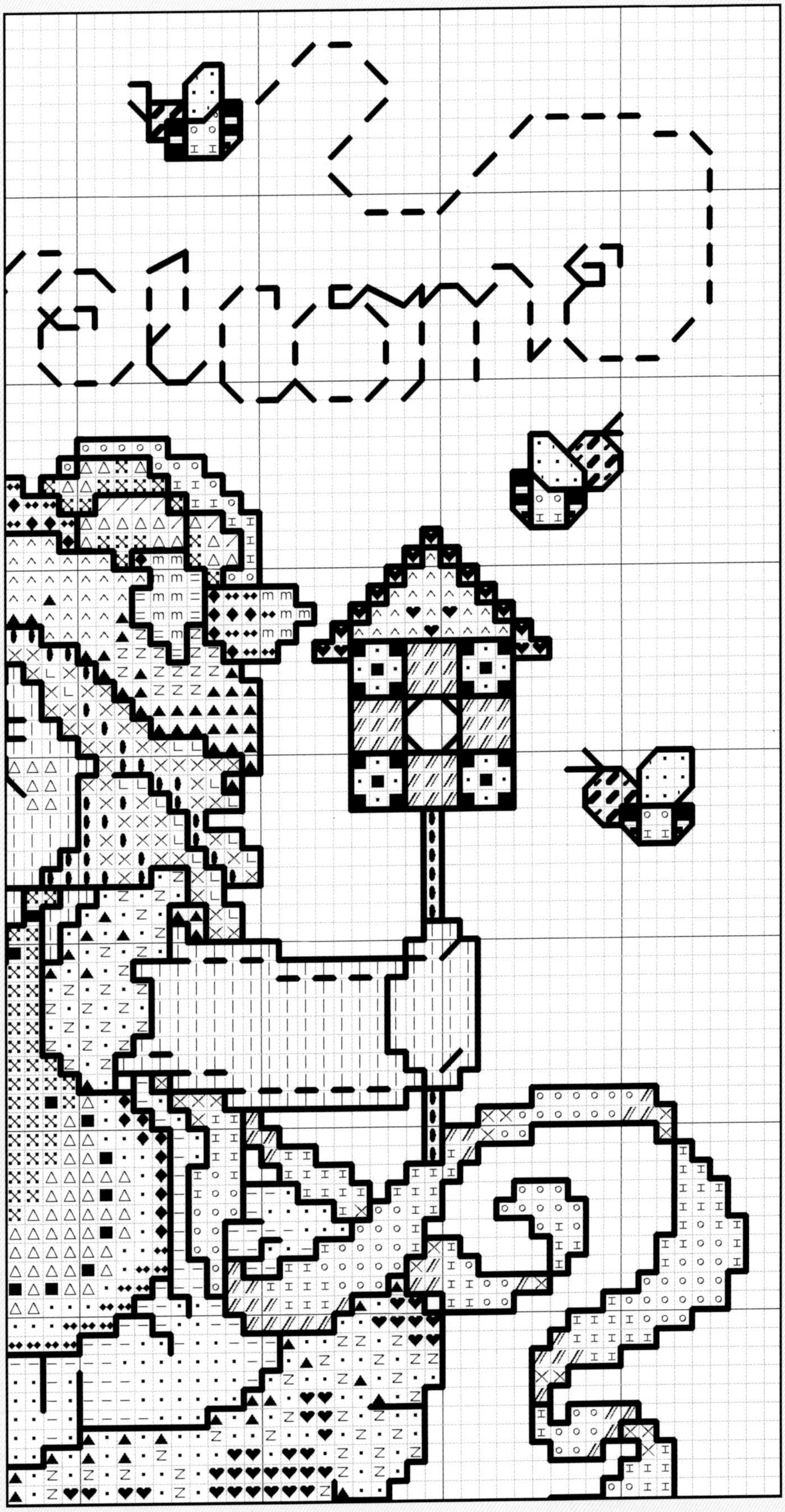

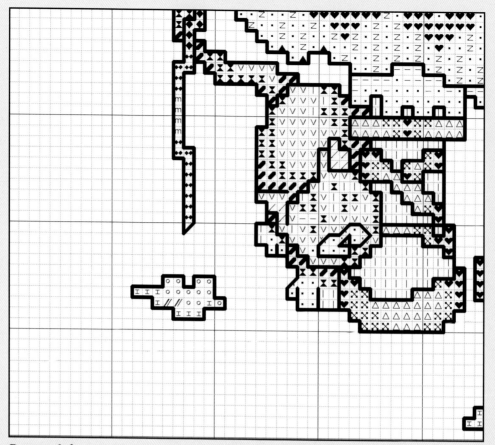

Bottom left

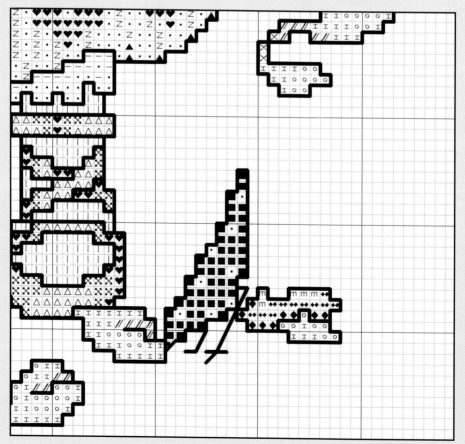

Bottom right

# The Tea Party

•Designed by Sandy Orton

Napkin stitched on ivory Jobelan, 28-ct, stitched over two threads, the finished design size is 1⅞" x 1⅞". The fabric was cut 12" x 12".

Tablecloth stitched on ivory Jobelan, 28-ct, stitched over two threads, the finished design size is 33⅞" x 33⅞". The fabric was cut 41¼" x 41¼".

Napkin Stitch Count: 27w x 27h
Tablecloth Stitch Count: 474w x 474h

| Sym | DMC | Description |
| --- | --- | --- |
| • | blanc | White |
| 6 | 223 | Shell Pink - med lt |
| Z | 224 | Shell Pink - lt |
| / | 225 | Shell Pink - vy lt |
| ✎ | 322 | Navy Blue - vy lt |
| ◆ | 434 | Brown - lt |
| ⌘ | 436 | Tan |
| I | 561 | Malachite - dk |
| ❚ | 648 | Beaver Grey - lt |
| ⨯ | 738 | Tan - vy lt |
| — | 746 | Off-White |
| ○ | 772 | Leaf Green - lt |
| ◓ | 922 | Copper - lt |
| ɪ | 966 | Baby Green - med |
| △ | 977 | Golden Brown - lt |
| L | 3072 | Beaver Grey - vy lt |
| ⑤ | 3325 | Baby Blue - lt |
| ● | 3346 | Hunter Green - med |
| ✖ | 3347 | Hunter Green - med lt |
| ♥ | 3721 | Shell Pink - med dk |
| ★ | 3755 | Baby Blue - med |
| ■ | 3799 | Charcoal Grey - dk |
| ✍ | 3816 | Celadon Green - med |

Blended Needle:

m      471 (2 strands) + 3348 (1 strand)

Backstitch: (1 strand except where noted)
   434 - flourishes (2 strands)
   801 - rabbits' heads, ears, hands, and feet; carrot and its indentation marks; "ground" marks near carrots
   221 - radishes and roots; teacups and saucers; pink portion of teapot
   319 - radish leaves; carrot leaves; cabbage table; green portions of teapot
   797 - dresses
   3799 - noses; apron; apron ties
   3799 - eyes and eyelashes (2 strands)

Models:
   Cross-stitch: 3 strands
   Backstitch: 1 strand except where noted

Napkin Materials: (for one napkin)
•Ivory sewing thread

Directions:
   1. Overcast or zigzag raw edges. Using three strands of floss, complete Carrot Design on page 55 in a lower right corner of the fabric square, ⅞" in from raw edges.
   2. For hems, fold raw edges under ¼" , fold edges under ¼" again, and press. Hand-stitch in place.

Tablecloth Materials:
•Ivory sewing thread

Directions:
   1. Overcast or zigzag raw edges. Using three strands of floss, complete The Tea Party Design on pages 55-58 in a lower right corner of the fabric square, 2¾" in from raw edges. To stitch the border, repeat section eleven times before stitching the corner section along the sides with the rabbits in the corner and twelve times for the remaining sides.
   2. For hems, fold raw edges under ⅞", fold edges under ⅞" again, mitering the corners. Press. Hand-stitch in place.

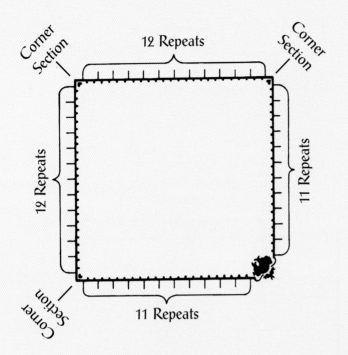

Corner Section

12 Repeats

Corner Section

12 Repeats

11 Repeats

Corner Section

11 Repeats

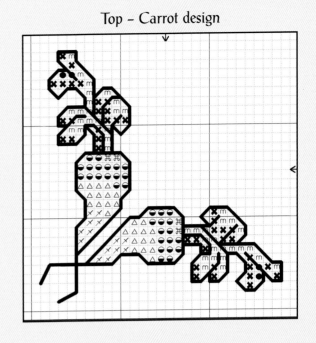

Top – Carrot design

Top left - The Tea Party Design

Corner Section

Repeat Section

Corner Section

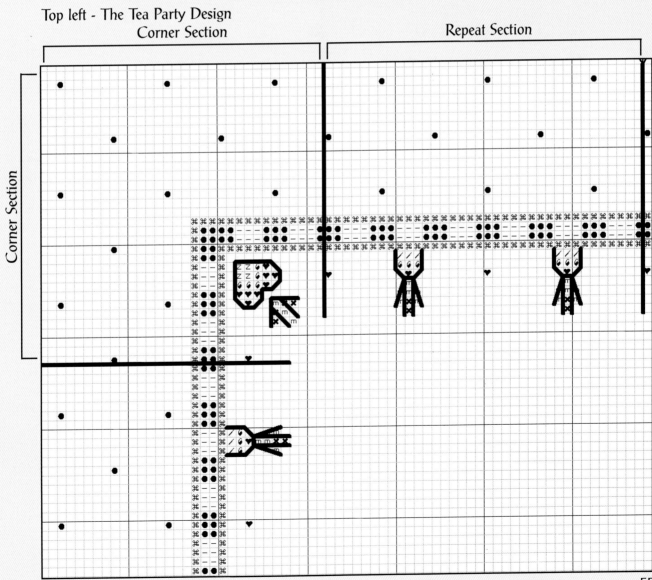

Repeat Section

Corner Section

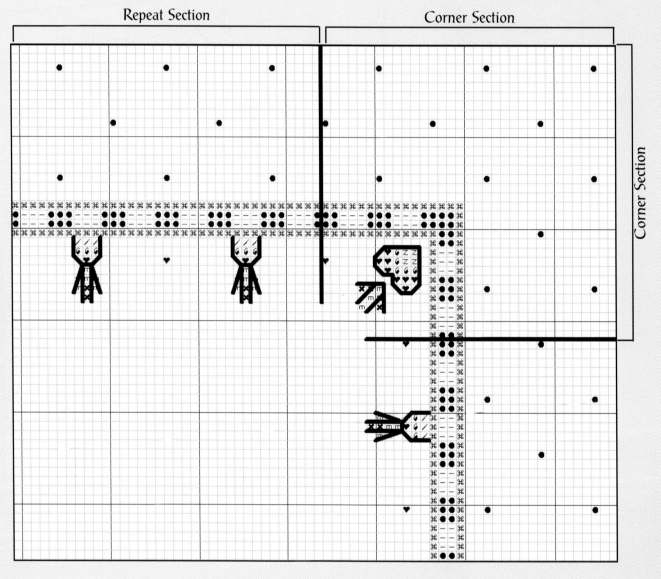

Corner Section

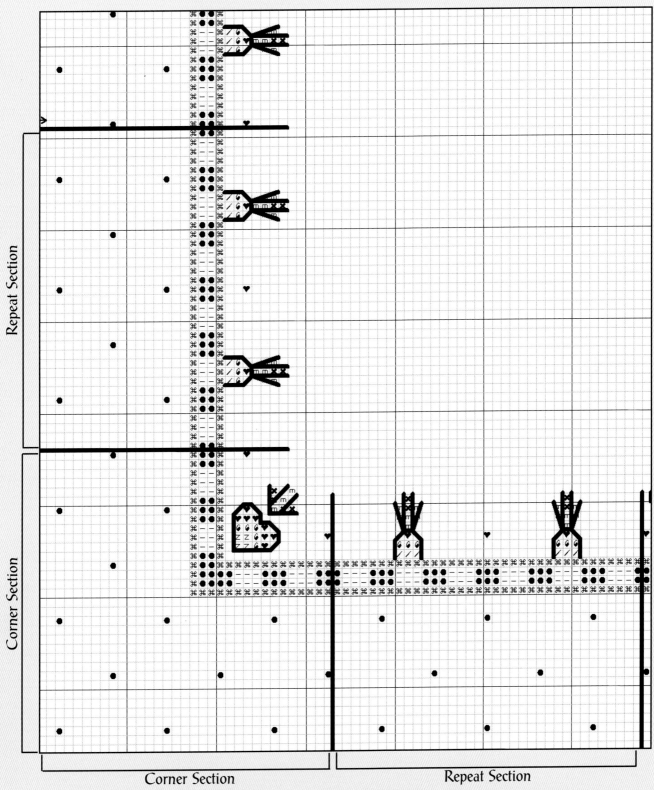

Bottom left - The Tea Party Design

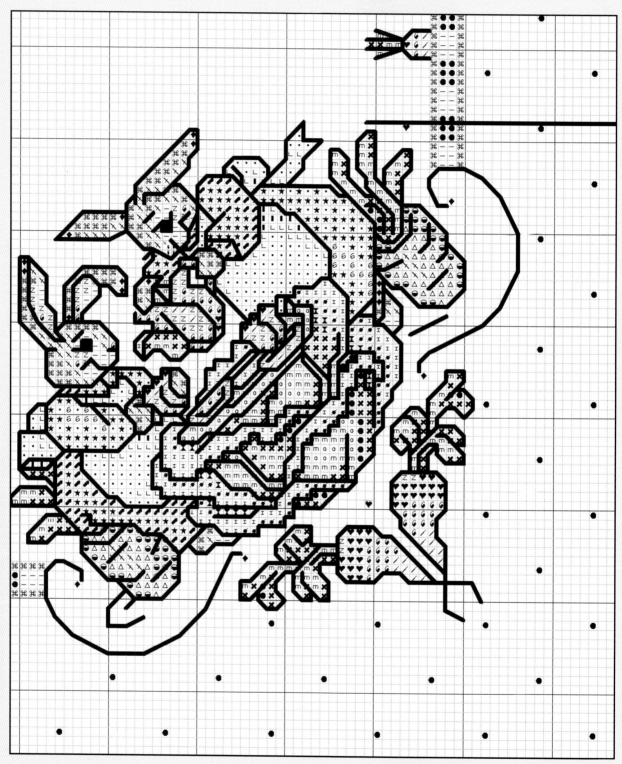

Bottom right - The Tea Party Design

# Glorious Cabbage

•Designed by Donna Kooler

Stitched on summer khaki Aida 14, the finished design size is 9" x 9". The fabric was cut 12" x 12".

Stitch Count: 126w x 126h

| Sym | DMC | Description |
|---|---|---|
| ♥ | 319 | Pistachio Green - dk |
| L | 472 | Avocado Green - vy lt |
| ✚ | 500 | Blue Green - vy dk |
| ◒ | 501 | Blue Green - dk |
| ★ | 502 | Blue Green - med dk |
| ✕ | 744 | Yellow - lt |
| ■ | 823 | Navy Blue - dk |
| ▲ | 833 | Green Gold - lt |
| ❢ | 987 | Forest Green - dk |
| ○ | 3053 | Grey Green - lt |
| ▪ | 3078 | Golden Yellow - vy lt |
| ⌘ | 3347 | Hunter Green - med lt |
| 2 | 3348 | Hunter Green - lt |
| m | 3363 | Leaf Green - dk |
| ✦ | 3750 | Antique Blue - vy dk |

Backstitch: (2 strands)
500 - leaves

Model:
Cross-stitch: 3 strands
Backstitch: 2 strands

Pillow Materials:
•⅜ yd two-toned green striped fabric
•Green sewing thread
•2" x 54" strip med-weight batting
•Polyester fiberfill

Directions:
•Use ½" seam allowance

1. Trim design fabric to ½" beyond stitching.

2. Cut green fabric into one square (use design fabric as pattern) and one 5" x 55" strip (ruffle) when pieced.

3. With right sides facing, sew short ends of strip together. With right sides out, fold strip in half lengthwise. Press.

4. To form shirred ruffle, lay batting strip inside fabric loop. Tack short ends of batting together.

5. Sew two lines of gathering stitches on ruffle unit, ¼" and ½" from raw edges. Gather to approximately 36".

6. Baste ruffle unit to right side of design fabric, matching raw edges.

7. Sew backing to pillow unit, right sides together, and leave a 4" opening on one side for turning. Remove all basting threads.

8. Turn pillow right sides out. Stuff pillow with fiberfill, taking care to fill the corners and slip-stitch opening closed.

"We can
taste,
see,
smell,
hear,
and touch
in a vegetable
garden.
Few art forms
offer that."

— Rosemary
Verey

Top right

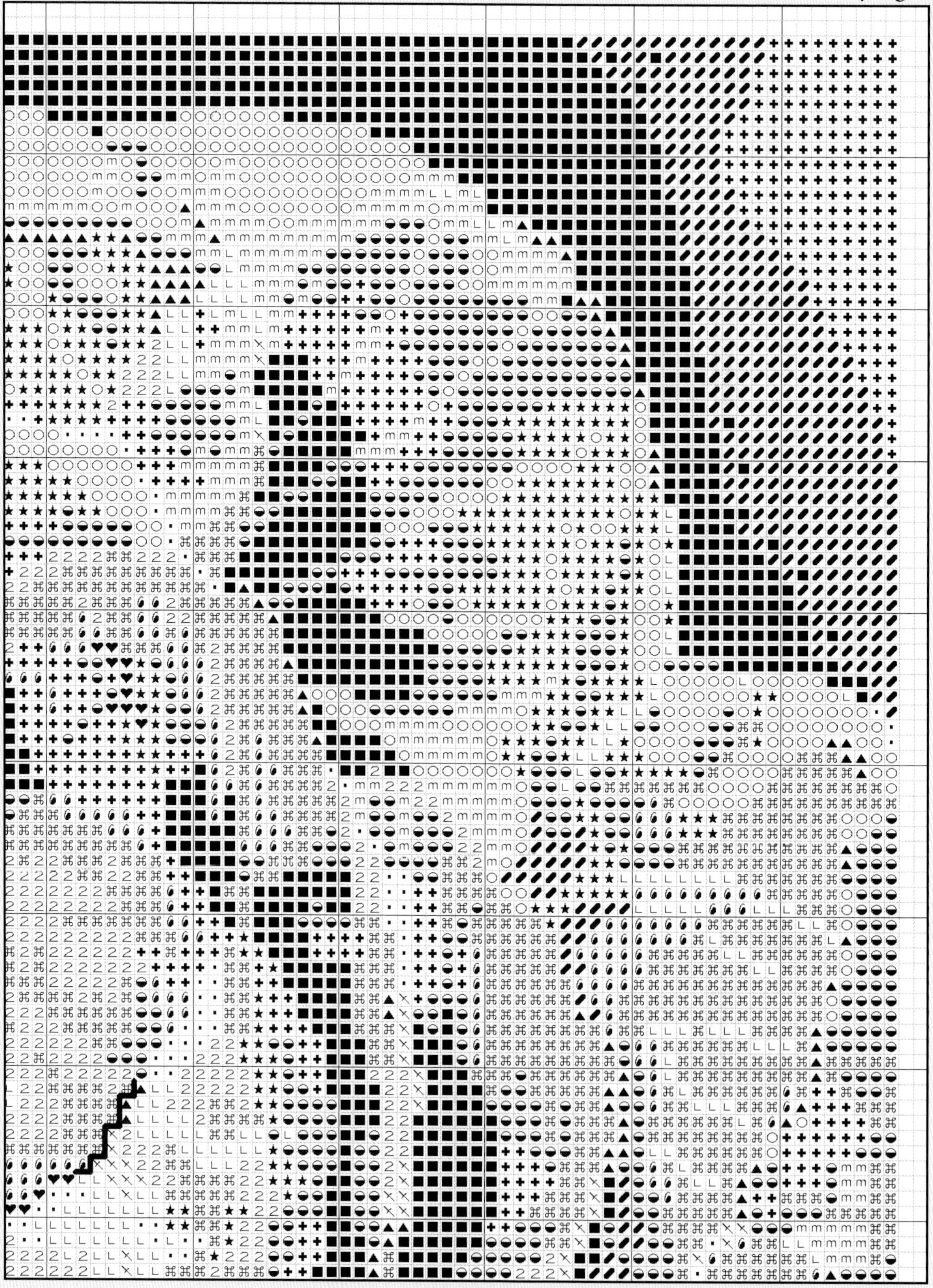

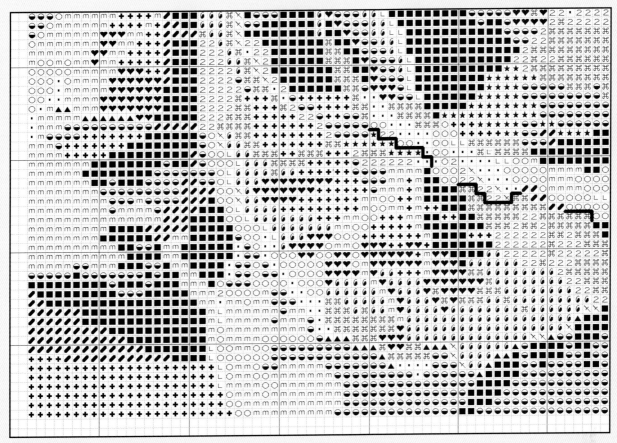

Bottom left

Bottom right

# Victorian Home

•Designed by Nancy Rossi

Stitched on antique white Aida 14, the finished design size is 8" x 9". The fabric was cut 17" x 19".

Stitch Count: 112w x 126h

| Sym | DMC | Description |
|---|---|---|
| . | blanc | White |
| ◆ | 221 | Shell Pink - dk |
| ■ | 310 | Black |
| ◔ | 320 | Pistachio Green - med lt |
| • | 434 | Brown - lt |
| ✕ | 471 | Avocado Green - lt |
| I | 472 | Avocado Green - vy lt |
| ◢ | 535 | Ash Grey - dk |
| ♥ | 602 | Cranberry - med |
| = | 613 | Drab Brown - lt |
| > | 642 | Beige Grey - med |
| - | 644 | Beige Grey - med lt |
| ▮ | 792 | Cornflower Blue - dk |
| ട | 793 | Cornflower Blue - med |
| ○ | 932 | Antique Blue - lt |
| △ | 951 | Pink Beige - lt |
| # | 957 | Geranium - lt |
| ✎ | 964 | Aqua - lt |
| ▲ | 3790 | Beige Grey - vy dk |
| ✕ | 3822 | Straw - lt |
| ◗ | 3830 | Terra Cotta - med dk |

Blended Needle:

| m | 3778 (2 strands) + 976 (1 strand) |
|---|---|
| ⁄⁄ | 436 (2 strands) + 976 (1 strand) |

Half Cross-stitch:

| L | 3747 (2 strands) |
|---|---|
| ✓ | 341 (4 strands) |

Backstitch: (1 strand except where noted)

310 - lamp post; glass chimney for lamp

221 - chimney; finials near steps; base of lightening rod; innermost diagonal lines of the two gables

320 - shrubs; stems and leaves of plants growing on fence; line on window boxes

792 - "Home Sweet Home" lettering in fence (2 strands)

792 - remaining portion of fence; blue roof; blue decorations on upper roof, porch, and base of turret

3790 - lamp bulb; diagonal shingle lines in turret roof; clapboard lines; outline of house, excluding roof areas; upper two roof lines of gables; leading lines in upper portions of windows; door; dark portions of columns; lower edge of window boxes; decorative diagonal lines (right-hand side only) on upper gable

642 - top of lamp post; internal reflection line in lamp chimney; lightening rod; turret roof ribs; windows; light portions of columns; upper vertical decorations in upper gable; decorative diagonal lines (left-hand side only) on upper gable; roof line above innermost roof line

French Knot: (3 strands)

792 - fence

Straight Stitch: (3 strands)

964 - sunray ornamentation above door

Model:

Cross-stitch: 3 strands

Backstitch: 1 strand, except where noted

Framed Piece Materials:

•10½" x 12⅜" frame

•Double-mat set with 8½" x 9⅜" opening

Directions:

1. Insert design fabric into frame and mat set.

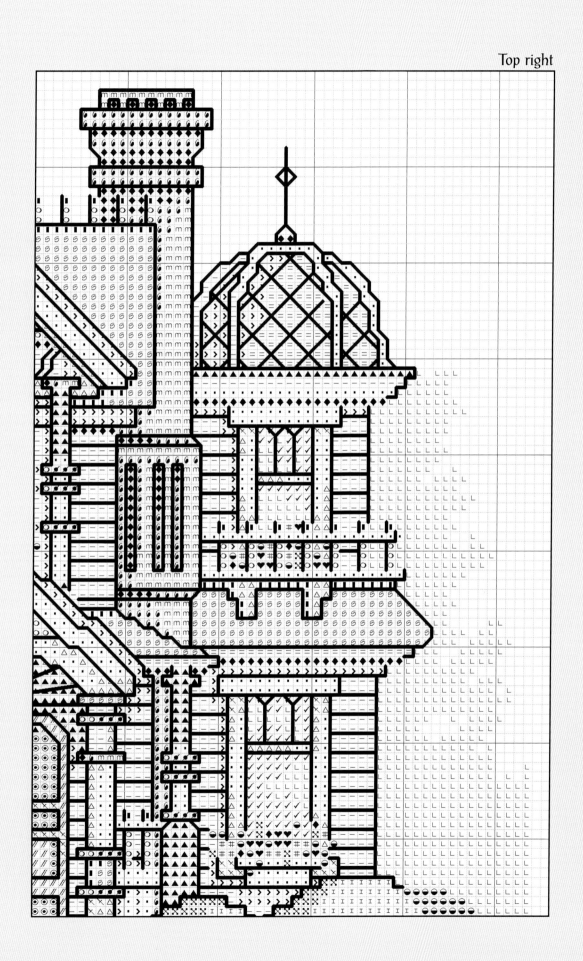

Bottom left

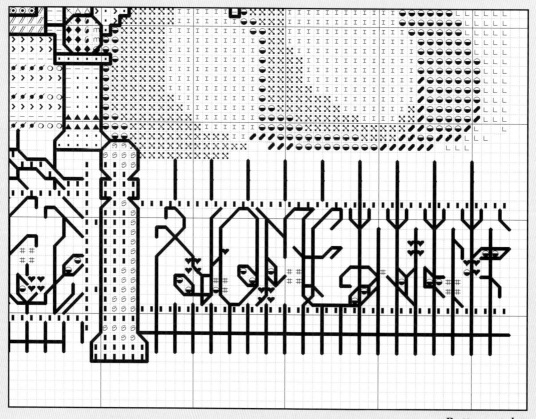

Bottom right

"A heavenly paradise
is that place
where all
pleasant fruits do flow.
Where cherries grow
which none may buy.
Till 'cherry-ripe' themselves
do cry."

– Thomas Campion

# Bear Tales

•Designed by Linda Gillum

Stitched on antique white Aida 14, the finished design size is 7⅞" x 9⅝". The fabric was cut 15" x 17".

Stitch Count: 111w x 134h

| Sym | DMC | Description |
|---|---|---|
| − | blanc | White |
| ● | 300 | Mahogany - vy dk |
| ■ | 310 | Black |
| 🌢 | 321 | Christmas Red |
| m | 402 | Mahogany - lt |
| ▲ | 413 | Pewter Grey - dk |
| ↑ | 434 | Brown - lt |
| = | 436 | Tan |
| ★ | 469 | Avocado Green - med |
| ◖ | 553 | Violet - med |
| ✕ | 606 | Orange Red - bright |
| ⤬ | 738 | Tan - vy lt |
| ∨ | 739 | Tan - ultra vy lt |
| ⲓ | 744 | Yellow - lt |
| # | 775 | Baby Blue - vy lt |
| ◆ | 797 | Royal Blue - med dk |
| ✓ | 798 | Delft Blue - dk |
| L | 799 | Delft Blue - med |
| ♥ | 816 | Garnet - med |
| ▮ | 839 | Beige Brown - dk |
| ◓ | 840 | Beige Brown - med |
| ⌘ | 841 | Beige Brown - lt |
| n | 842 | Beige Brown - vy lt |
| ◣ | 920 | Copper - med dk |
| • | 922 | Copper - lt |
| / | 945 | Pink Beige - med |
| x | 958 | Aqua - dk |
| ⫽ | 964 | Aqua - lt |

| Sym | DMC | Description |
|---|---|---|
| ^ | 3340 | Melon - med |
| H | 3348 | Hunter Green - lt |
| $ | 3364 | Leaf Green - med |
| > | 3608 | Fuchsia - med |
| I | 3609 | Fuchsia - lt |
| ▪ | 3756 | Baby Blue - ultra vy lt |
| ✚ | 3821 | Straw - med |

Backstitch: (1 strand)
  799 - wallpaper stripes
  922 - chicks' beaks
  310 - bears' eyes, noses, and mouths; rabbit's nose; border
  839 - dk brown bear
  300 - chicks; lt and med colored bears; rabbit (not tail or muzzle)
  413 - everything else

French Knot: (1 strand)
  310 - chicks' eyes

Model:
  Cross-stitch: 3 strands
  Backstitch: 1 strand

Framed Piece Materials:
  •11⅛" x 12⅞" frame (2⅛"-wide)

Directions:
  1. Insert design fabric into frame.

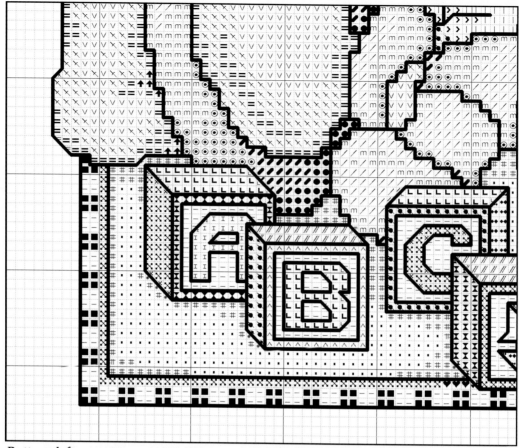

Bottom left

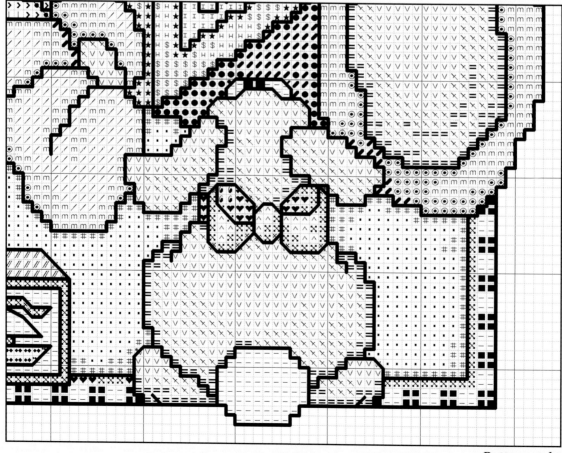

# Home Sweet Home

•Designed by Sandy Orton

Stitched on light sand Edinburgh linen, 36-ct, stitched over two threads, the finished design size is 9⅛" x 3¾". The fabric was cut 14" x 31".

Stitch Count: 165w x 67h

| Sym | DMC | Description |
|---|---|---|
| • | 223 | Shell Pink - med lt |
| ■ | 902 | Garnet - vy dk |
| ✕ | 3041 | Antique Violet - med |
| + | 3052 | Grey Green - med |
| ● | 3721 | Shell Pink - med |
| ▲ | 3740 | Antique Violet - dk |

Blended Needle:

| | | |
|---|---|---|
| ⊡ | 3828 + 021BF | Hazelnut Brown - med and Kreinik blending filament |

Backstitch: (2 strands)

902 - shadow lines for capital letters

3041 - shadow lines for lower case letters; continuation lines for inner flourishes of capital letters

Couched Straight Stitch:

221 antique gold fine braid (#8 braid) - couched with 021BF copper Kreinik blending filament (2 strands)

Lazy Daisy: (1 strand except where noted)

902 - inside capital letters (2 strands)

221 antique gold fine braid - around outside of saying

Model:

Cross-stitch: 2 strands

Backstitch: 2 strands

Pillow Materials:

•⅝ yd burgundy crushed velour upholstery fabric
•Burgundy sewing thread
•⅝ yd lightweight muslin
•Polyester fiberfill
•Heavy-duty carpet thread
•White dressmaker's chalk

Directions:

•Use ½" seam allowance.

1. Trim design fabric to 10½"x 28½" with design centered.

2. Fold design fabric lengthwise with right side of design inside and sew long sides together, leaving a 5" opening at center. Press seam open. With seam at center back, sew each end closed. Turn right side out and press back of design fabric. Set aside.

3. Cut two 19" x 22½" pieces each of velour and muslin. With right sides together, sew around all four edges of velour fabric, leaving a 5" opening along one 22½" side (bottom). Repeat for muslin pieces.

4. Using dressmaker's chalk, mark one horizontal line on both sides of the velour pillow, 7½" from bottom seam line. Mark another horizontal line 4" above and parallel to first lines. For the gathering lines, use heavy thread and hand sew along each marked horizontal line, using a ½"-long running stitch. Bring each of these running stitch threads to the right side of the pillow and leave 6"-long tails. Turn pillow right sides out and set aside.

5. Turn muslin pillow right side out. Lightly stuff pillow with polyester fiberfill and hand-stitch opening closed. Insert into velour pillow and hand-stitch opening closed.

6. Pull running stitch threads to gather until central area of pillow is about 27" in diameter. Secure threads.

7. Place design fabric band around central area of pillow with right side out and ends overlapping ½". Hand-stitch ends together.

Top right

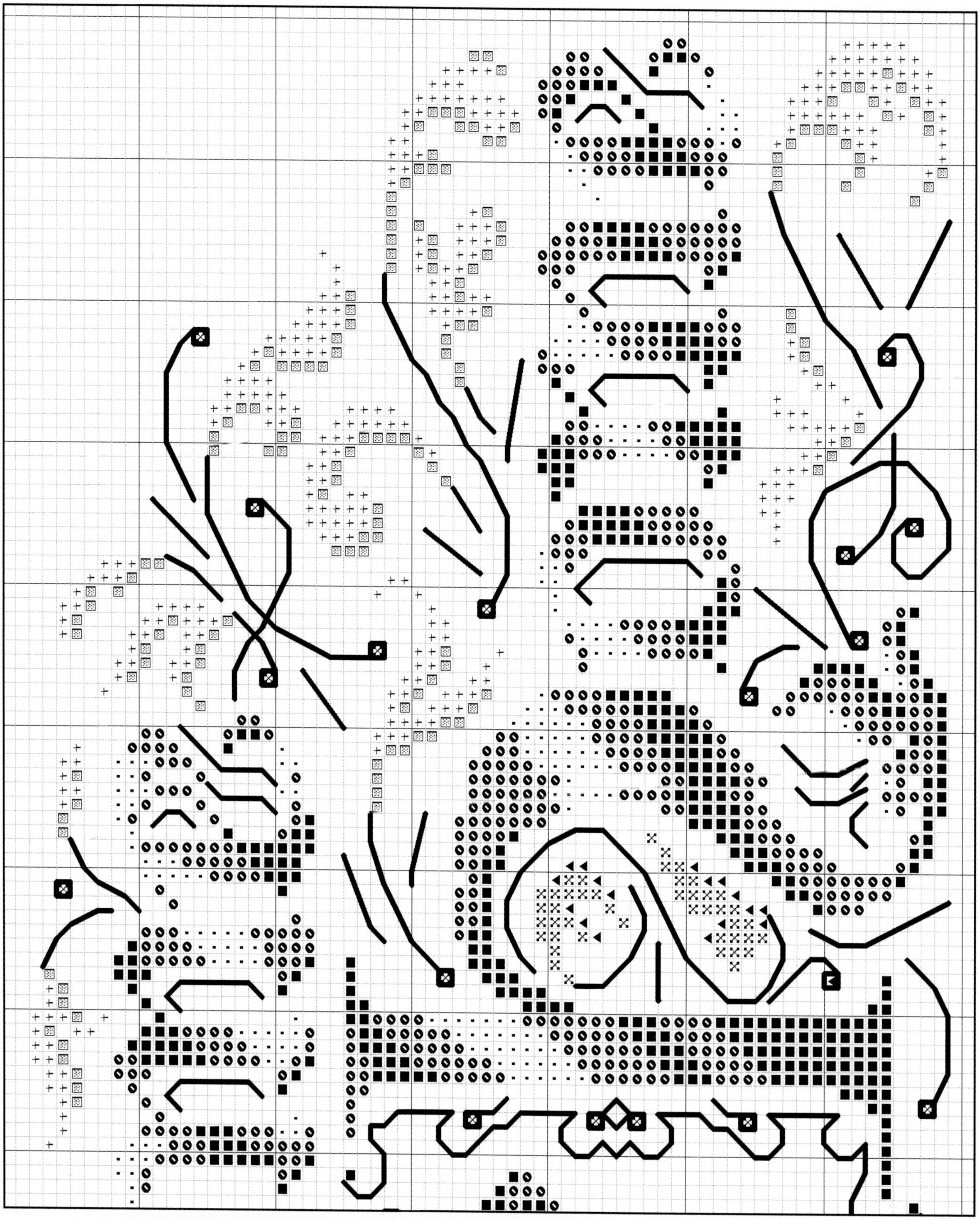

# Cats, Bats, n' Pumpkins

•Designed by Barbara Baatz

Stitched on sweatshirt using 8" x 10" waste canvas, 10-ct., the finished design size for Halloween Cat is 8¾" x 7⅛" and Pilgrim Cat is 8½" x 5¾".

Halloween Cat Stitch Count: 86w x 71h
Pilgrim Cat Stitch Count: 85w x 56h

## Halloween Cat

| Sym | DMC | Description |
|---|---|---|
| ▪ | blanc | White |
| ● | 310 | Black |
| ✎ | 400 | Mahogany - dk |
| ✇ | 413 | Pewter Grey - dk |
| × | 415 | Pearl Grey |
| ♥ | 550 | Violet - vy dk |
| ✍ | 552 | Violet - dk |
| = | 553 | Violet - med |
| ⊙ | 699 | Christmas Green - vy dk |
| > | 702 | Kelly Green |
| ʜ | 704 | Chartreuse - bright |
| ⌘ | 720 | Rust - med |
| ƽ | 741 | Tangerine -med |
| ↑ | 742 | Tangerine - lt |
| ° | 743 | Yellow - med |
| ʟ | 745 | Yellow - vy lt |
| m | 760 | Salmon - med lt |
| ⊖ | 792 | Cornflower Blue - dk |
| # | 793 | Cornflower Blue - med |
| / | 794 | Cornflower Blue - lt |
| ▌ | 820 | Royal Blue - vy dk |
| x | 839 | Beige Brown - dk |
| ◆ | 890 | Pistachio Green - vy dk |
| ⊥ | 900 | Burnt Orange - dk |
| ▲ | 920 | Copper - med dk |
| ★ | 970 | Pumpkin - med |

Backstitch: (1 strand except where noted)
  310 - bats; cat; cat's paws, eyes, nose, and mouth
  310 - line between candle and flame (2 strands)
  550 - ribbon

890 - leaves; vines
820 - cat's hat
839 - outlines of pumpkin's nose and mouth; candle holder; stars
938 - pumpkin; outline of eyes
413 - candle; candle's flame

Straight Stitch: (4 strands)
  blanc - highlights in cat's eyes
  743 - highlights in bats' eyes

## Pilgrim Cat

| Sym | DMC | Description |
|---|---|---|
| ▪ | blanc | White |
| ● | 310 | Black |
| ✎ | 400 | Mahogany - dk |
| ✇ | 413 | Pewter Grey - dk |
| ✔ | 414 | Steel Grey - dk |
| × | 415 | Pearl Grey |
| ▐ | 435 | Brown - vy lt |
| □ | 437 | Tan - lt |
| ↑ | 597 | Turquoise - med |
| ▲ | 640 | Beige Grey - dk |
| m | 642 | Beige Grey - med |
| / | 644 | Beige Grey - med lt |
| △ | 676 | Old Gold - lt |
| ⊙ | 699 | Christmas Green - vy dk |
| > | 702 | Kelly Green |
| ʜ | 704 | Chartreuse - bright |
| ⌘ | 720 | Rust - med |
| ⊖ | 729 | Old Gold - med |
| ƽ | 741 | Tangerine - med |
| x | 839 | Beige Brown - dk |
| ◆ | 890 | Pistachio Green - vy dk |
| ★ | 970 | Pumpkin - med |
| ♥ | 3809 | Turquoise - dk |
| ʟ | 3823 | Yellow - ultra vy lt |

Backstitch: (1 strand except where noted)
  839 - pumpkin stem
  938 - pumpkin
  310 - cat; cat's paws, tail, eyes, nose, and mouth; hat; crow; feathers

640 - yellow squash

890 - leaves; vines

3809 - feather shaft (4 strands)

Straight Stitch: (4 strands)

blanc - highlight in cat's and crow's eyes

## Models:

Cross-stitch: 4 strands

Backstitch: 1 strand except where noted

## Holiday Sweatshirts Materials:

•Sweatshirts (blue for Halloween Cat, jade green for Pilgrim Cat)

•8" x 10" piece of waste canvas (10 count)

•8" x 10" piece of lightweight nylon interfacing

•White sewing thread

Directions:

1. Position Halloween Cat design 2¾" (3" for Pilgrim Cat) from neck seam and centered side to side.

2. With the design centered, baste the waste canvas to the front and the interfacing to the inside front of the sweatshirt.

3. Stitch design.

4. Moisten the waste canvas and gently remove the threads of the waste canvas from under and around the design.

5. Trim the interfacing around the design.

Top - Pilgrim Cat

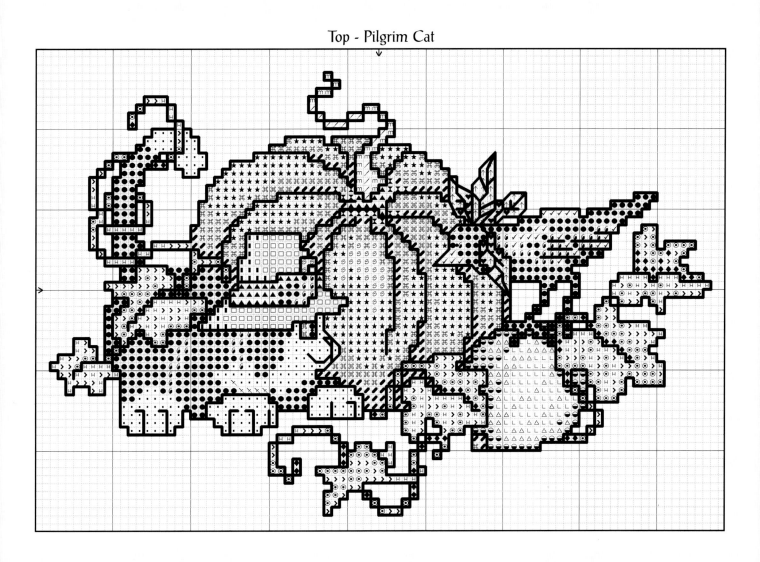

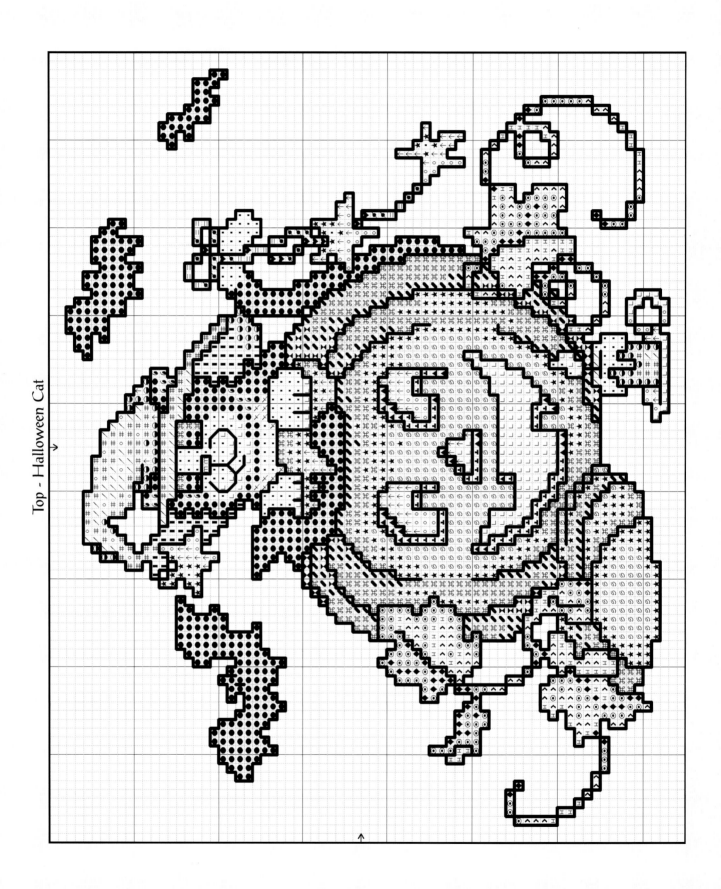

Top - Halloween Cat

# Chrysanthemums

•Designed by Barbara Baatz

Stitched on country flax Anne Cloth, 18-ct, stitched over two threads, the finished design size is 12½" x 15½". The fabric for afghan was cut 1¼ yds.

Stitch Count: 112w x 140h

| Sym | DMC | Description |
|-----|-----|-------------|
| • | blanc | White |
| x | 300 | Mahogany - vy dk |
| ⋋ | 351 | Coral - med |
| ✍ | 502 | Blue Green - med dk |
| ↑ | 742 | Tangerine - lt |
| – | 745 | Yellow - vy lt |
| ♥ | 815 | Garnet - med dk |
| ★ | 817 | Coral Red - vy dk |
| ▲ | 824 | Blue - vy dk |
| ✕ | 826 | Blue - med dk |
| ◆ | 895 | Hunter Green - vy dk |
| ⊥ | 900 | Burnt Orange - dk |
| ╱ | 919 | Copper - dk |
| ✚ | 921 | Copper - med |
| = | 932 | Antique Blue - lt |
| > | 977 | Golden Brown - lt |
| ◖ | 989 | Forest Green - med |
| ⦿ | 3340 | Melon - med |
| m | 3346 | Hunter Green - med |
| o | 3348 | Hunter Green - lt |
| / | 3753 | Antique Blue - ultra vy lt |
| # | 3776 | Mahogany - med lt |
| ■ | 3799 | Charcoal Grey - dk |
| I | 3813 | Blue Green - med lt |
| ^ | 3824 | Melon - vy lt |

Backstitch: (2 strands)
   300 - berry stems; center of white flower
   920 - small melon-orange bud and flower
   815 - small dk orange flowers
   932 - white flower
   921 - yellow flower
   3799 - berries
   895 - leaves

Model:
   Cross-stitch: 4 strands
   Backstitch: 2 strands

Afghan Materials:
   •Ecru sewing thread

Directions:

   1. Machine-zigzag raw edges of afghan to prevent fraying.

   2. Position design in the lower left corner of afghan, ¼" from the inner decorative woven line on the left-hand side of the second row of squares and ¼" from the inner decorative woven lines on the bottom of the second row of squares. This provides one row of unstitched squares at the left and bottom of the design.

   3. Stitch design, using 4 strands for the cross-stitches and 2 strands for the backstitches.

   4. Sew small zigzag line 2⅜" to the outside of the outer decorative woven line from the design and continuing around the afghan, allowing five full squares by seven full squares on the inside of the afghan.

   5. Trim the afghan so that there are the maximum but same number of threads on the sides and top and bottom from the inside zigzag line.

   6. Fringe to zigzag lines. Using an overhand knot, tie fringe in groups of six threads. At the corners use three threads from each side. If some compensation is necessary in the number of threads per tie, do this several ties from the corners.

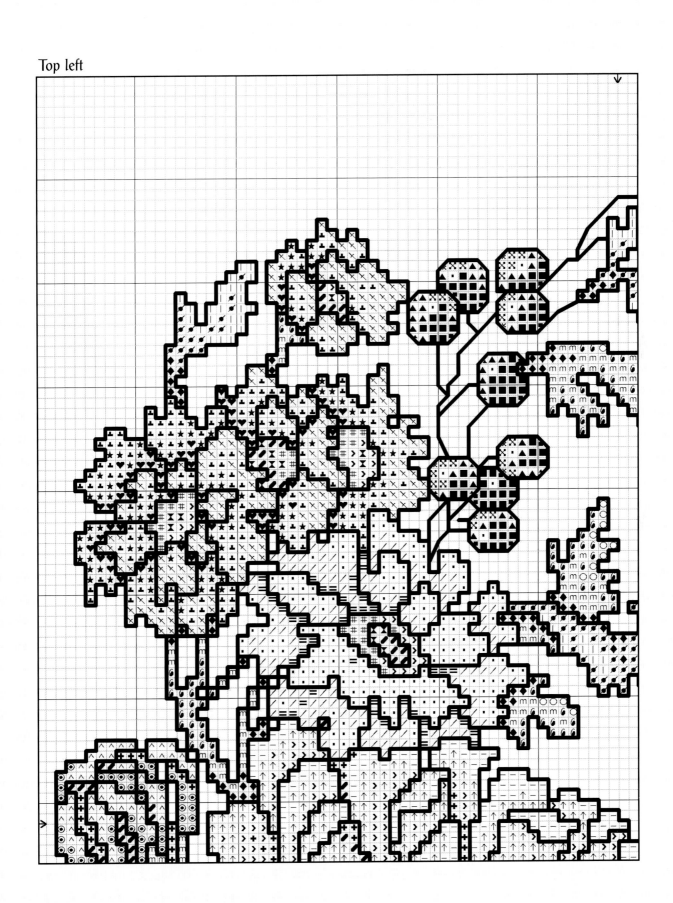

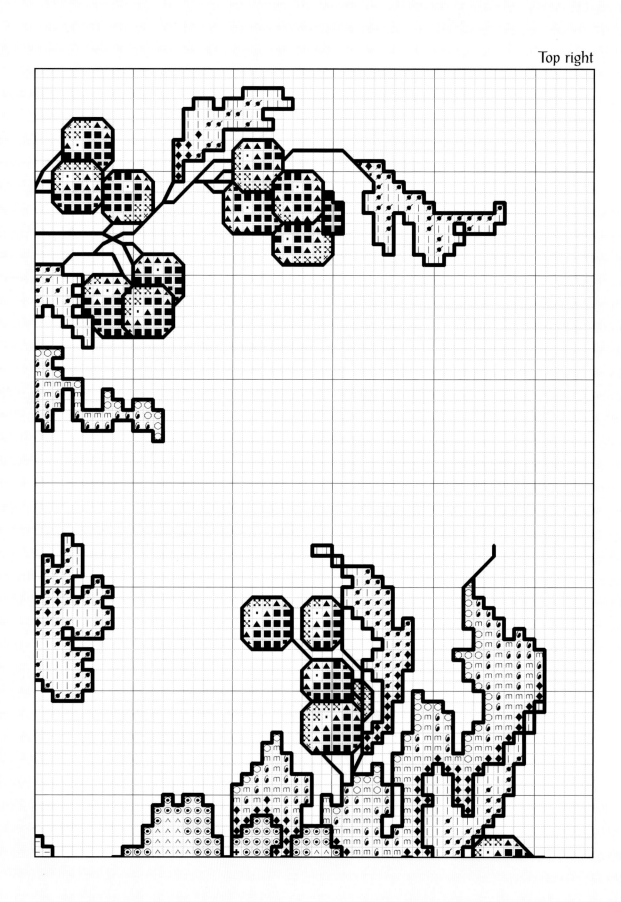

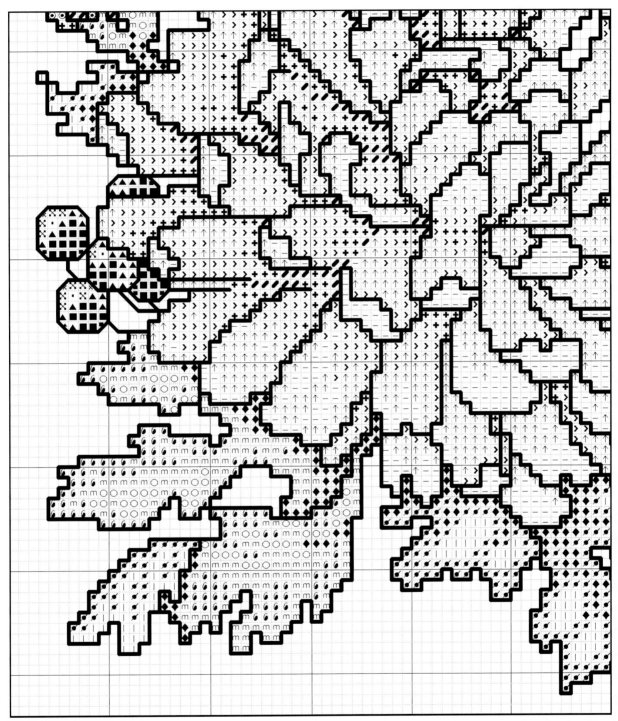

Bottom left

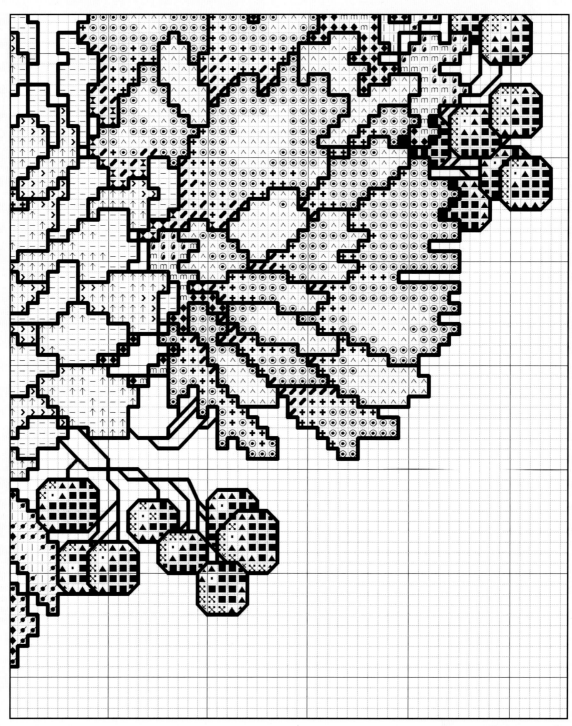

Bottom right

"I saw old
Autumn
in the misty
morn
stand shadowless
like silence,
listening to
silence."

— Thomas Hood

"The Autumn
sky is
endless—
endless—
stretching
toward dusk
and night."

— Tu Fu

94

# Holly Jolly Snowmen

•Designed by Linda Gillum

Completed Holly Jolly Snowmen designs* stitched on one 8" x 11" sheet of white perforated plastic, 14 mesh, allowing a minimum of four "squares" between each snowman. The finished design size is 9¼" x 6¾".

Stitch Count: 130w x 94h

| Sym | DMC | Description |
|-----|-----|-------------|
| · | blanc | White |
| ◑ | 209 | Lavender - dk |
| △ | 211 | Lavender - lt |
| ■ | 310 | Black |
| ♥ | 321 | Christmas Red |
| ✓ | 437 | Tan - lt |
| ⌘ | 606 | Orange Red - bright |
| x | 702 | Kelly Green |
| I | 704 | Chartreuse - bright |
| H | 743 | Yellow - med |
| L | 745 | Yellow - vy lt |
| = | 747 | Sky Blue - vy lt |
| ₲ | 772 | Leaf Green - lt |
| m | 775 | Baby Blue - vy lt |
| ● | 796 | Royal Blue - dk |
| ✖ | 798 | Delft Blue - dk |
| − | 818 | Baby Pink |
| > | 927 | Grey Blue - med |
| ○ | 928 | Grey Blue - lt |
| ✍ | 964 | Aqua - lt |
| ▲ | 975 | Golden Brown - dk |
| ✎ | 996 | Electric Blue - med |
| ✔ | 3341 | Melon - lt |
| ✚ | 3607 | Fuchsia - dk |
| / | 3609 | Fuchsia - lt |
| 2 | 3824 | Melon - vy lt |
| □ | 3825 | Rust - vy lt |
| ★ | 5282 | Gold Metallic |

Backstitch: (1 strand except where noted)

Birdhouse Snowman: See (1)

  310 - black portions of birds; snowman's eye and mouth

  321 - red bird; scarf; birdhouse pole; heart patch; pompom on blue bird

  931 - snowman's outline

  975 - nose; twig arms; yellow portions of cap

  413 - everything else

Angel Snowman: See (2)

  310 - snowman's eyes, nose, and mouth

  321 - berries; ribbon

  975 - yellow plaid heart; star

  700 - holly leaves

  931 - everything else

Snowman with Reindeer: See (3)

  310 - snowman's eyes, nose, and mouth; reindeer's eyes and mouth

  700 - holly leaves; pocket; string on jingle bells; bell strap on reindeer

  975 - hat band; scarf; reindeer's body and horns; small and medium jingle bells

  796 - hat; checkered cuffs

  321 - berries; reindeer's nose; heart; coat

  413 - mittens

  931 - snowman's outline

Snowman with Tree: See (4)

  975 - star; tree trunk

  700 - tree; stocking stripes

  321 - red portion of cap; heart; mittens; red portion of sled

5282 - line work inside hearts on sled

310 - hearts on sled (2 strands)

310 - snowman's eyes, nose, and mouth; shoe (not sole); remaining portions of sled

931 - snowman's outline

413 - everything else

## Snowman with "Joy" Sign: See (5)

310 - snowman's eyes, nose, and mouth

5282 - string for ornaments

321 - "Joy"; scarf; mittens; heart; lollipop; candy cane and stripes; stripes on pole for sign

796 - coat and pocket

931 - snowman's outline; outline of sign; sign pole

413 - everything else

## "Let it Snow" Snowman: See (6)

413 - mouse; saying; ornaments and strings

310 - snowman's mouth; outlines around checkerboard border; bird's eye; black portions of bird

975 - bird's outline and beak; snowman's nose

700 - mittens

321 - red portion of hat not covered by snow

931 - everything else

## Models:

Cross-stitch: 3 strands

Backstitch: 1 strand except where noted

## Ornaments Materials:

•1 yd ⅛"-wide red satin ribbon (for ornament hangers)

•Six 4" squares of small Christmas print cotton fabric

•White fabric glue

•Small scissors with sharp points

•Optional accessories (see photo for placement): 6mm brass jingle bells; 9mm red jingle bells; ¼" white and blue buttons; star button; heart button; 5, 7, and 9mm pompoms; 4mm magenta silk ribbon; green floral wire; 24-gauge gold tone beading wire; 8mm wooden beads; gold-colored glass seed beads.

*If accessories are to be used, omit stitching the halo, jingle bells, and wire in snowman's hand, treetop star, and string of lights (fill in the "Joy" sign and cap with appropriately colored cross-stitches). For the buttons, pompoms, bow, and small jingle bells, sew these accessories directly over their stitched areas.

## Directions:

1. Using scissors, carefully cut around each snowman, leaving one "thread" free between stitching and cut line.
Optional: Attach accessories.

2. Cut red ribbon into six 6" lengths. Fold ribbon lengths in half and glue cut ends to center back of each ornament, ½" from top edge.

3. Lightly glue fabric square to ornament (wrong sides facing). Trim fabric to design edge.

*"King Winter's in the wood
I saw him go
Crowned with a coronet
Of crystal snow."*

*— Eileen Mathias*

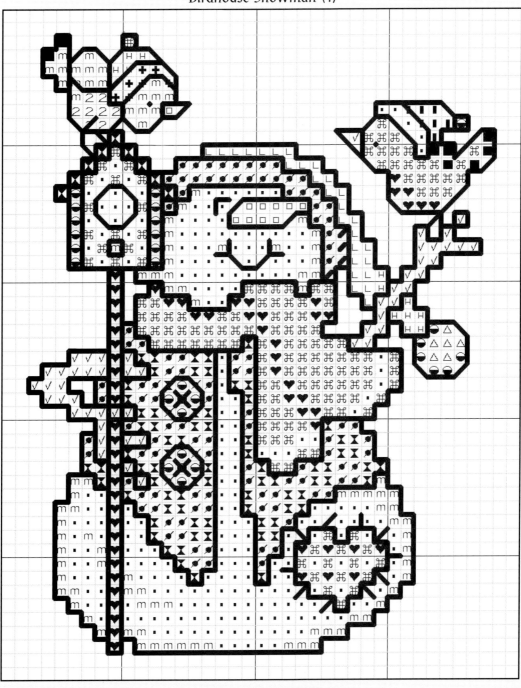

## Angel Snowman (2)

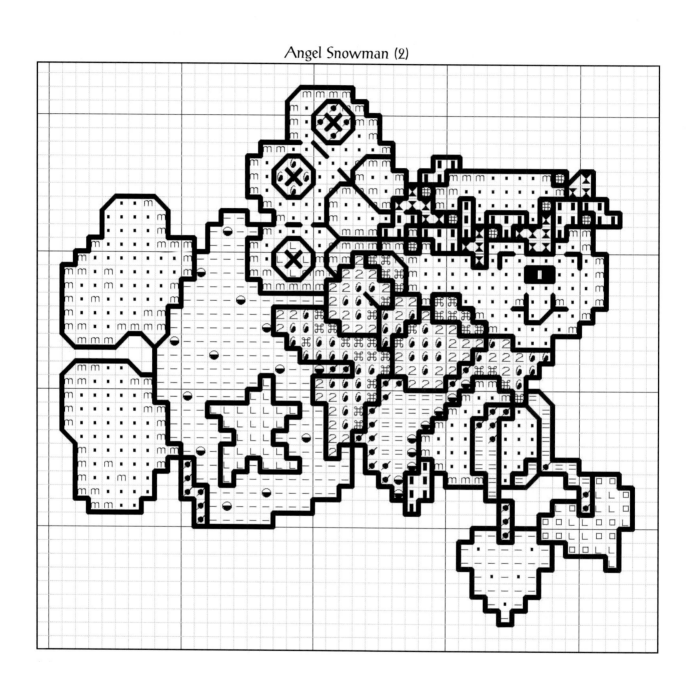

Snowman with Reindeer (3)

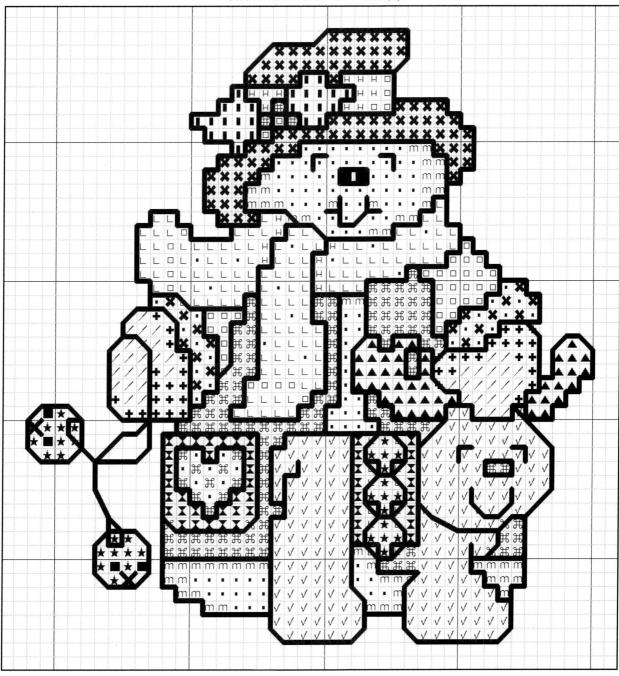

Snowman with Tree (4)

Snowman with "Joy" Sign (5)

"Let it Snow" Snowman (6)

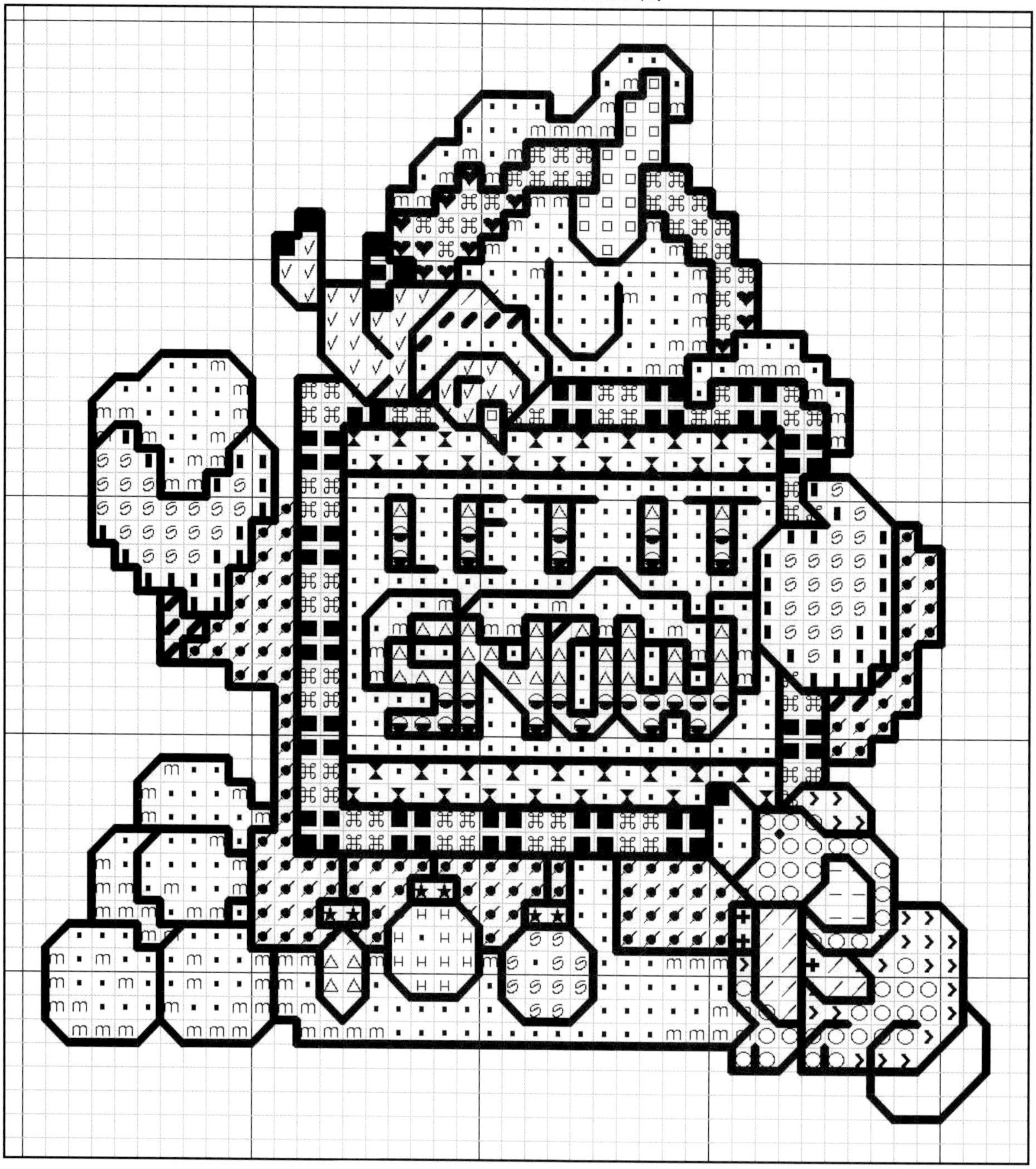

# Folk Santa

•Designed by Sandy Orton

Completed red Santa stitched on antique white Aida 11, the finished design size is 4⅝" x 8½". The fabric was cut 13" x 16".

Completed yellow Santa stitched on antique white Aida 14, the finished design size is 3⅝" x 6¾". The fabric was cut 11" x 14".

Completed blue Santa stitched on antique white Aida 18, the finished design size is 2⅞" x 5¼". The fabric was cut 7" x 10".

Stitch Count: 51w x 94h

| Sym | DMC | Description |
|---|---|---|
| | | (Alternate Robe Colors) |
| • | blanc | White |
| ■ | 310 | Black |
| ✕ | 349 | Coral - dk |
| | | (yellow - 725; blue - 799) |
| I | 351 | Coral - med |
| | | (yellow - 3078; blue - 3753) |
| o | 351 | Coral - med |
| | | (cheeks only) |
| ⊥ | 413 | Pewter Grey - dk |
| = | 414 | Steel Grey - dk |
| ᕽ | 415 | Pearl Grey |
| ▲ | 434 | Brown - lt |
| 𝟨 | 435 | Brown - vy lt |
| // | 437 | Tan - lt |
| ★ | 562 | Malachite - med |
| – | 754 | Peach - lt |
| m | 758 | Terra Cotta - lt |
| ● | 816 | Garnet - med |
| | | (yellow - 783; blue - 798) |
| ◆ | 902 | Garnet - vy dk |
| | | (yellow - 869; blue - 796) |
| 2 | 3348 | Hunter Green - lt |
| ♥ | 3818 | Emerald Green - ultra vy dk |

Backstitch: 1 strand except where noted

310 - red and yellow Santa's top eyelids; ermine marks; bear's nose (2 strands)

310 - blue Santa's top eyelids; Santa's and bear's eyes; gloves; boots; sack; bear's mouth and eyebrows

3818 - tree; belt

898 - bear; tree trunk

632 - Santa's nose

413 - fur trim; beard; eyebrows; mustache

902 - red robe and hat (yellow - 869; blue - 796)

## Note:

1. Sometimes a diagonal backstitch line will obscure a symbol beneath it. Choose a logical floss color closest to it.

## Models:

Cross-stitch: 11-ct (4 strands - red Santa)

14-ct (3 strands - yellow Santa)

18-ct (2 strands - blue Santa)

Backstitch – except where noted

11-ct (2 strands)

14-ct (1 strand)

18-ct (1 strand)

## Pillow Doll Set Materials:

•¼ yd dk green plaid fabric
•2 yds 3⁄16"-wide dk green cording
•White, dk green, and invisible sewing thread
•4" x 6" lightweight poster board for each Santa
•5-oz. fishing weights
(red Santa - 2; yellow Santa - 1; blue Santa - 1)
•Polyester fiberfill
•Tracing paper
•White fabric glue
•Hot glue and glue gun
•Embellishments and miniatures
(see photo for ideas)

## Directions:

•See Santa Pattern and Base on page 105.

1. Fold tracing paper in half and align fold with straight side of Santa pattern. Trace and cut out. Repeat for base.

2. Using appropriately sized Santa pattern, place pattern on wrong side of design with feet ¼" above base line and centered side to side. Lightly trace around pattern on wrong side of design fabric. Add ½" seam allowance to all sides and cut out design fabric.

3. Using design fabric for pattern, cut one green fabric piece (backing).

4. For Base: using appropriately sized Santa base pattern, cut out one from poster board. Cut one from green fabric, adding ½" beyond pattern. Center right side of fabric over poster board, pull edges to back and glue (fabric glue). Center and hot glue fishing weight(s) to back of base.

5. With right sides facing, sew design and backing pieces together, leaving base open. Clip curves, turn right sides out, and fill with fiberfill.

6. Hand-stitch cording around Santa at seam line, starting and stopping at raw edges. Trim cording even with raw edges of Santa and apply white glue to ends to prevent fraying.

7. Hand tack base to Santa, adding more stuffing if necessary.

8. With the invisible thread, hand tack embellishments (jingle bells, buttons, brass charms, beads, ribbon bows, and dollhouse miniatures) to Santa dolls. See photo for placement and ideas.

9. Repeat for each size Santa.

Santa Pattern
Enlarge 120%

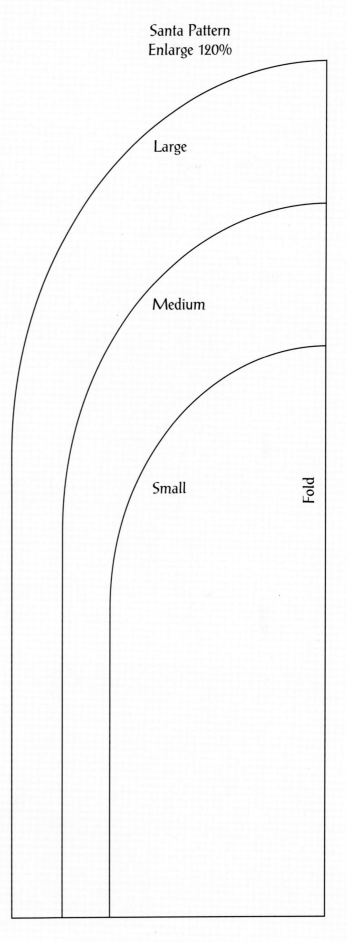

Base
Enlarge 120%

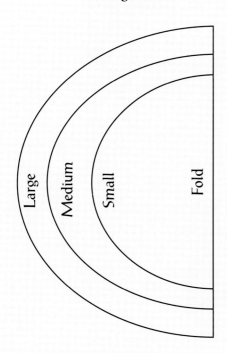

# Unicorn Carousel

•Designed by Linda Gillum

Stitched on forget-me-not blue Jobelan, 28-ct, stitched over two threads, the finished design size is 7¾" x 9⅝". The fabric was cut 16" x 18".

Stitch Count: 108w x 134h

| Sym | DMC | Description |
|-----|-----|-------------|
| ▪ | blanc | White |
| > | 211 | Lavender - lt |
| ♥ | 301 | Mahogany - med |
| ■ | 310 | Black |
| ╱ | 317 | Pewter Grey |
| ⊥ | 318 | Steel Grey - lt |
| ◓ | 402 | Mahogany - lt |
| # | 415 | Pearl Grey |
| ◖ | 604 | Cranberry - lt |
| ✓ | 605 | Cranberry - vy lt |
| = | 745 | Yellow - vy lt |
| L | 747 | Sky Blue - vy lt |
| – | 762 | Pearl Grey - vy lt |
| ς | 775 | Baby Blue - vy lt |
| ◆ | 798 | Delft Blue - dk |
| ✚ | 813 | Blue - med |
| ▮ | 913 | Emerald Green - med lt |
| H | 945 | Pink Beige - med |
| ^ | 951 | Pink Beige - lt |
| Y | 955 | Emerald Green - vy lt |
| ★ | 959 | Aqua - med |
| m | 964 | Aqua - lt |
| ⌘ | 3325 | Baby Blue - lt |
| ▲ | 3608 | Fuchsia - med |
| ◗ | 3609 | Fuchsia - lt |
| △ | 3756 | Baby Blue - ultra vy lt |
| ✖ | 3776 | Mahogany - med lt |
| ● | 002P | Kreinik Metallic-Gold Cable |

## Blended Needle:

| / | blanc (3 strands) + 032 Kreinik blending filament (1 strand) |
| ↑ | 745 (3 strands) + 091 Kreinik blending filament (1 strand) |
| ⊥ | 3609 (2 strands) + blanc (1 strand) |
| ○ | 211 (2 strands) + blanc (1 strand) |

## Smyrna Cross:

798 (1 strand) + 006 Kreinik blending filament (1 strand) - ornamental drape on unicorn's breast; snowflakes above unicorn

## Elongated Smyrna Cross:

798 (1 strand) + 006 Kreinik blending filament (1 strand) - ornamental drape on unicorn's rear

## French Knot: (1 strand except where noted)

317 - top of flag poles

798 (1 strand) + 006 Kreinik blending filament (1 strand) - ornamental drape on unicorn's breast

## Backstitch: (1 strand except where noted)

blanc - four small radial arms in small snowflake "round" (3 strands)

002P - lightening

310 - Father Frost's eyes; unicorn's eyebrow

813 - wind

301 - owls' eyes, beaks, and feet; moon; brown border; pole; Father Frost's eyebrows, nose, cheeks, and lips; brown and yellow portions of saddle; unicorn's eye; circle surrounding castle

798 - clouds; rain drops; snowflakes; snow; melting snow; snowflakes at bottom; lt blue border; trees; castle; path to castle; snowflake "rounds"

798 (1 strand) + 006 Kreinik blending filament (1 strand) - ornamental drape on unicorn's breast; snowflakes above unicorn

317 - everything else

## Model:

Cross-stitch: 3 strands except where noted

Backstitch: 1 strand except where noted

## Framed Piece Materials:

•11⅞" x 13¾" frame with 1½"-wide liner with 9" x 10⅞" opening

1. Insert design
fabric into frame
and liner set.

Top

Bottom

# Cats, Books, & Candle

•Designed by Nancy Rossi

Stitched on sand Cashel linen 28-ct, stitched over two threads, the finished design size is 8" x 10". The fabric was cut 12" x 14".

Stitch Count: 112w x 140h

| Sym | DMC | Description |
|---|---|---|
| ▪ | blanc | White |
| ✦ | 221 | Shell Pink - dk |
| ∨ | 301 | Mahogany - med |
| ★ | 309 | Rose - dk |
| ■ | 310 | Black |
| ◆ | 319 | Pistachio Green - dk |
| н | 327 | Red Violet - dk |
| ✕ | 356 | Terra Cotta - med |
| ✍ | 367 | Pistachio Green - med |
| ✓ | 413 | Pewter Grey - dk |
| // | 415 | Pearl Grey |
| ◣ | 420 | Hazelnut Brown - dk |
| ✕ | 422 | Hazelnut Brown - lt |
| ◣ | 451 | Shell Grey - dk |
| m | 470 | Avocado Green - med lt |
| – | 472 | Avocado Green - vy lt |
| ▲ | 791 | Cornflower Blue - vy dk |
| = | 793 | Cornflower Blue - med |
| ◗ | 839 | Beige Brown - dk |
| + | 906 | Parrot Green - med |
| ⇧ | 975 | Golden Brown - dk |
| I | 3047 | Yellow Beige - lt |
| ○ | 3078 | Golden Yellow - vy lt (1 strand) |
| ◖ | 3721 | Shell Pink - med dk |
| ▽ | 3743 | Antique Violet - vy lt |
| ⊥ | 3776 | Mahogany - med lt |
| ⊕ | 3778 | Terra Cotta - med lt (1 strand) |
| ɪ | 3821 | Straw - med |
| < | 3825 | Rust - vy lt (1 strand) |

Blended Needle:

| Z | 402 (2 strands) + 977 (1 strand) Golden Brown blend |
|---|---|
| ^ | 902 (2 strands) + 838 (1 strand) Dk Garnet blend |
| ♥ | 945 (2 strands) + 3827 (1 strand) Lt Golden Brown blend |

Backstitch: (1 strand)

3721 - black kitten's nose

975 - black kitten's chin; orange kitten's outline; multi-colored kitten's outline on right side from ear to tail

413 - black kitten's outer outline and internal fur marks; orange kitten's toes and nose; dk book outlines; candle; "India"

310 - black and orange kitten's eyes; ink bottle

839 - whiskers; remaining book outlines; candlestick; plant pot; remaining outline for multi-colored kitten

319 - leaves; vines

838 - shelves; sides and top of bookcase; design motifs on bookcase front

Straight Stitch: (1 strand except where noted)

839 - lines on edges of books

413 - lines across book spines

415 - hair lines in orange kitten's ears (2 strands)

## Note:

1. A diagonal backstitch line obscures the symbol for a full cross-stitch beneath it. This full cross-stitch is symboled as fractional stitches (same symbols) on either side of the backstitch line. Stitch the cross-stitch as a full stitch and then place the backstitch line diagonally over the top of the stitch.

## Model:

Cross-stitch: 3 strands except where noted
Backstitch: 1 strand

## Framed Piece Materials:

•8⅞" x 10½" frame with ½"-wide liner

## Directions:

1. Insert design fabric into frame and liner set.

Top left

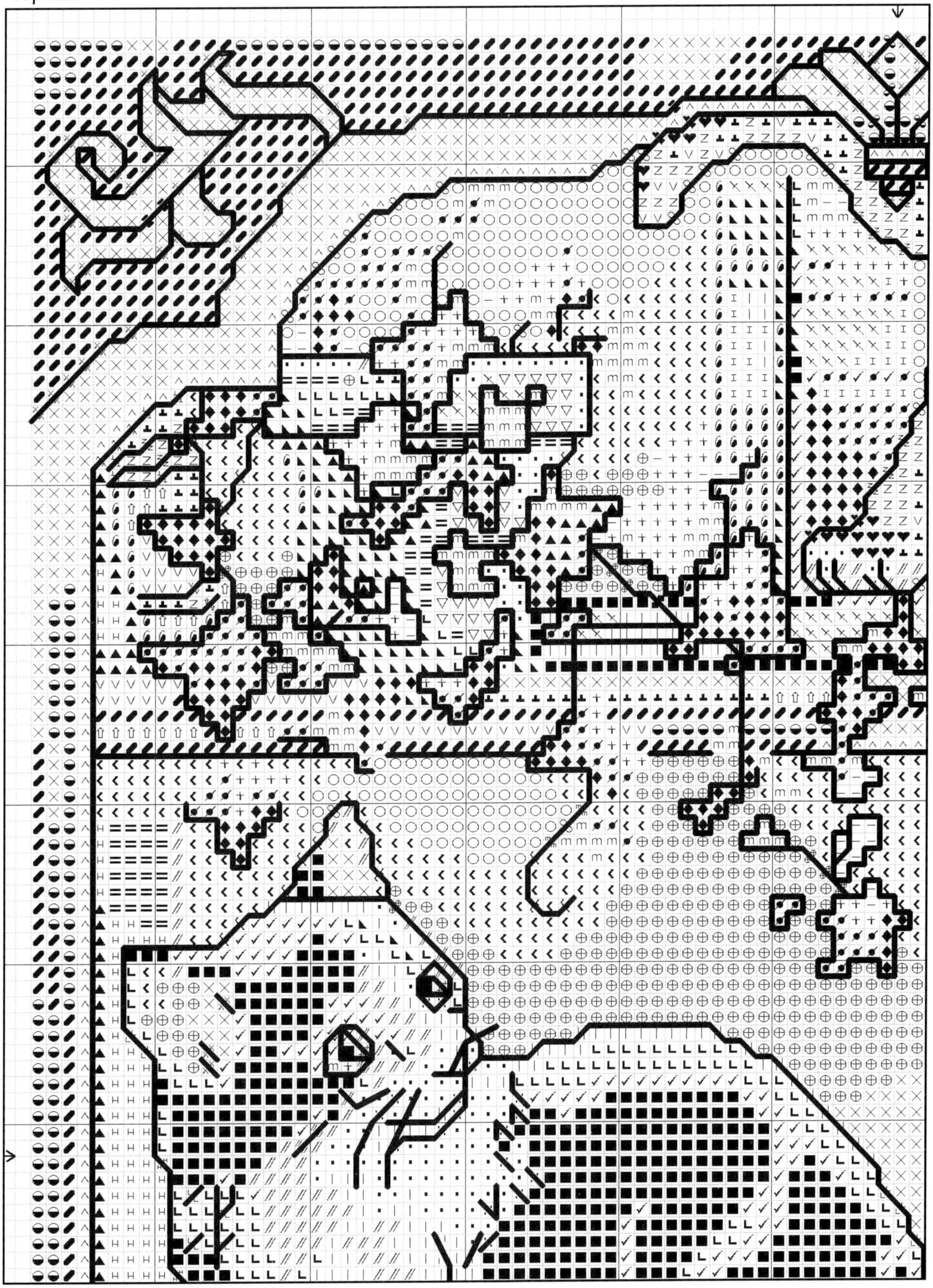

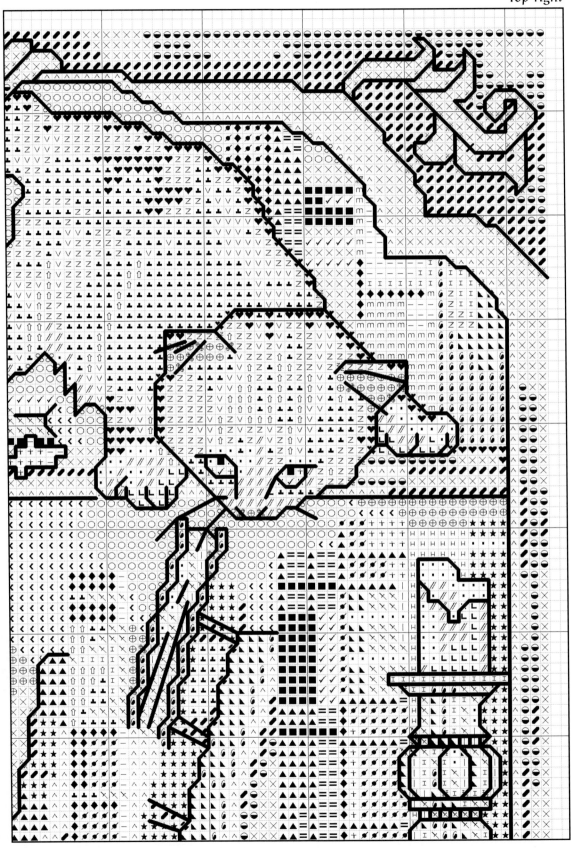

114

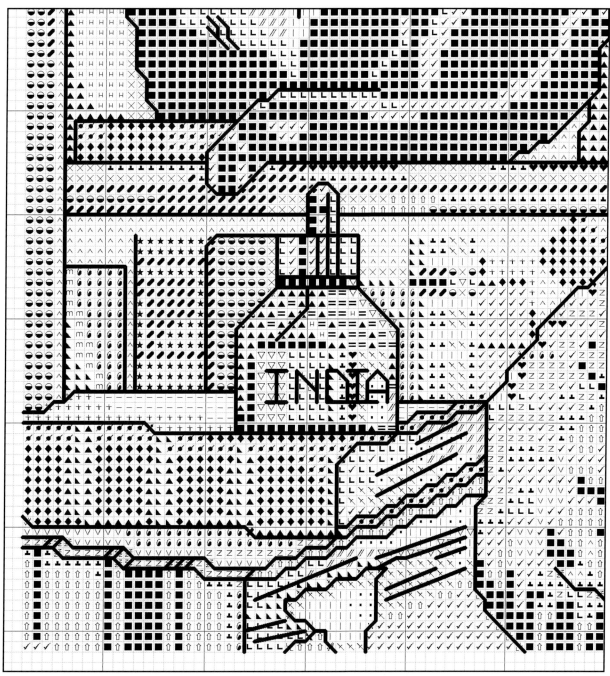

Bottom left

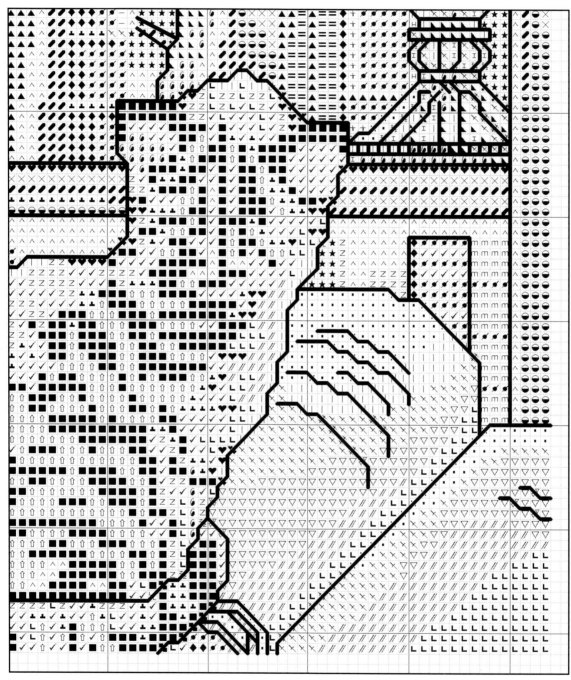

Bottom right

# Button, Button!

•Designed by Sandy Orton

Stitched on summer khaki Cashel linen 28-ct, stitched over two threads, the finished design size is 9¾" x 5½". The fabric was cut 15" x 11½".

Stitch Count: 136w x 76h

Note:
When stitching with overdyed floss, each individual cross-stitch must be completed before proceeding to the next one.

| Sym | Overdyed Floss | Description |
|-----|------|-------------|
| ○ | 184 | Summer Peach (Needle Necessities) |
| ★ | No number | "Dried Thyme" (Sampler Threads) |
| ▮ | 128 | Serengeti (Needle Necessities) |
| ◆ | No number | "Midnight" (Sampler Threads) |
| m | 113 | Tapestry Blue (Needle Necessities) |
| 2 | 123 | Bear Brown (Needle Necessities - *stitch button box in vertical rows*) |

Backstitch: (2 strands)
    113 - "Bachelor's Button"
    Midnight - "Button Box"; "Button, Button who's got the"
    128 - thread and tassels; "Cute as a Button"
    123 - hands
    Button Placement is indicated by black dots

Model:
    Cross-stitch: 3 strands
    Backstitch: 2 strands

Pillow Materials:
    •17 white pearl buttons* (specialty shapes: one ½"
moon, three ½" hearts, one ¾" bird, one ⅜" oval; rounds: six ⅜" dia, four ⅛" dia, one ½" dia)
    •2 mottled blue buttons* (½" dia)
    •8 mottled brown buttons* (four ⅜" dia, four ⅝" dia)
    •1 abalone button (1" dia)
    •½ yd upholstery-weight pastel plaid fabric
    •½ yd upholstery-weight blue gingham fabric
    •12" x 7½" piece of polyester fleece
    •Ecru sewing thread
    •Polyester fiberfill
    *Or use any contemporary or antique buttons in sizes and colors which will coordinate with the cross-stitch design
    Or use a purchased pillow (applique to center front and complete Step 5)

Directions:
    •Use ½" seam allowance.
    1. Using photograph and chart as guides, sew buttons to design fabric. Use Summer Peach floss to sew the heart buttons near hands. Use Tapestry Blue floss for remaining pearl and blue buttons. Use Dried Thyme floss for abalone button, and Serengeti floss for brown buttons.
    2. With design centered, trim design fabric to 12" x 7½". Baste design fabric to fleece.
    3. From plaid fabric, cut two strips 3½" x 12", two strips 3½" x 12½", and one piece 17" x 12½" (backing).
    4. Sew a plaid strip to top and bottom of design unit. Sew remaining strips to sides of design unit.
    5. Using 4 strands of remaining skein of Bear Brown floss, sew ¼" deep buttonhole stitches ³⁄₁₆" apart completely around the design fabric.
    6. Cut and piece blue gingham fabric to make a 6" x 90" strip. With right sides facing, sew short ends together forming a loop. Press seam open.
    7. With wrong sides facing and aligning long edges, press ruffle unit.
    8. Sew gathering stitches ¼" and ½" from long raw edges and gather to approximately 59".
    9. Matching raw edges, sew ruffle to design unit.
    10. With right sides together, sew design unit to backing, leaving a 3" opening. Turn pillow right sides out.
    11. Stuff pillow with fiberfill, taking care to fill the corners and slip-stitch opening closed.

BACHELOR'S BUTTON

Button'st the a Button

BACHELOR'S BUTTON

# Floral Fiesta

•Designed by Barbara Baatz

Stitched on soft white Abby Cloth 18-ct, stitched over two threads, the finished design size is 14" x 14". The fabric was cut 1¼ yds.

Stitch Count: 126w x 126h

| Sym | DMC | Description |
|-----|-----|-------------|
| △ | 210 | Lavender - med |
| ∪ | 211 | Lavender - lt |
| ■ | 310 | Black |
| ◣ | 321 | Christmas Red |
| ★ | 501 | Blue Green - dk |
| ✕ | 502 | Blue Green - med dk |
| < | 503 | Blue Green - med |
| ● | 550 | Violet - vy dk |
| ✐ | 552 | Violet - dk |
| ♥ | 606 | Orange Red - bright |
| ◤ | 640 | Beige Grey - med dk |
| ○ | 644 | Beige Grey - med lt |
| ✔ | 676 | Old Gold - lt |
| н | 741 | Tangerine - med |
| ▲ | 781 | Topaz - dk |
| ✆ | 783 | Christmas Gold |
| ✖ | 815 | Garnet - med dk |
| ▪ | 818 | Baby Pink |
| L | 822 | Beige Grey - lt |
| ← | 890 | Pistachio Green - vy dk |
| ⌘ | 947 | Burnt Orange - med |
| > | 956 | Geranium - med |
| ◉ | 957 | Geranium - lt |
| ⊥ | 987 | Forest Green - dk |
| m | 989 | Forest Green - med |
| Z | 3325 | Baby Blue - med lt |
| / | 3348 | Hunter Green - lt |
| ✕ | 3753 | Antique Blue - vy lt |

Backstitch: (2 strands)
310 - tulip stamens
327 - violet flowers
433 - tendrils; base of nasturtium bud
501 - blue-green leaves
815 - tulip, peony, and nasturtium flowers
986 - yellow-green leaves

Model:
Cross-stitch: 4 strands
Backstitch: 2 strands

Afghan Materials:
•White sewing thread

Directions:
1. Cross-stitch Floral Fiesta design over two threads on the Abby Cloth, using four strands of floss for the cross-stitches and two strands for the backstitches. The shaded bands on the chart indicate a thick band (3 threads woven closely together) and one additional thread on the fabric. Treat this grouping of 3 + 1 threads as a two normal threads.

2. Trim the design fabric 7¼" from the outer band on all four sides.

3. Withdraw the 44th thread from the outer band on all four sides.

4. Using the zigzag stitch, machine-stitch over the adjacent two threads on the design side from the withdrawn thread.

5. To fringe, withdraw threads from the raw edges to the zigzag line on all four sides.

Note: Top right quadrant is grid only and contains no stitching.

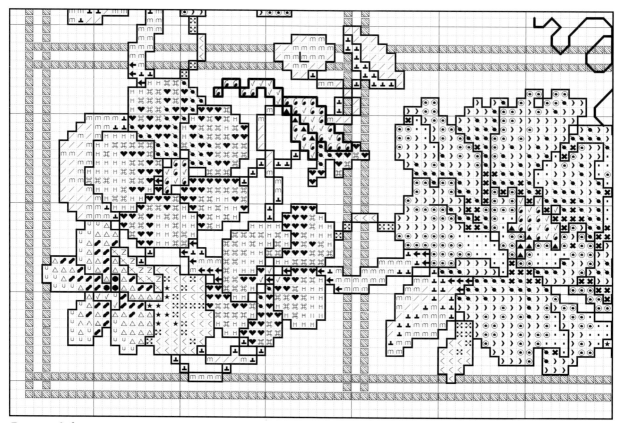

Bottom left

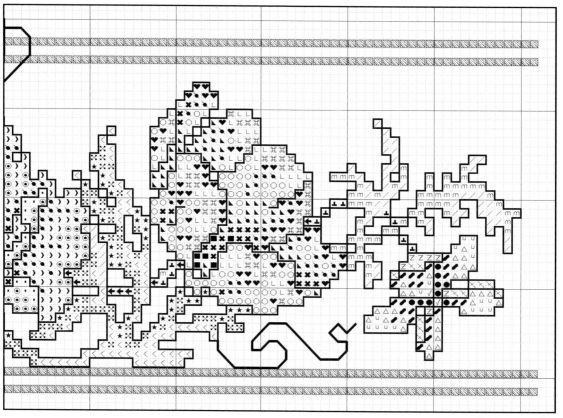

Bottom right

124

"Be brave.
Nature smiles in spring,
and laughs in summer,
and yawns in autumn,
but now she is weeping;
And with her tears
she waters life,
hidden under the earth.
Sleep,
for this white blanket
which makes us cold,
keeps the seeds warm."

– Kahlil Gibran

# General Instructions

## Backstitch

Use backstitches for all outlines or other design lines.

Pull the needle through at the point marked "A". Go down one opening to the right, at "B". Come back up at "C". Go down one opening to the right at "A".

## Buttonhole Stitch

Buttonhole stitches create a distinct pattern and are especially effective on edges. There they serve as a tool for outlining as well.

Bring needle up at A go down at B, and come up at C, looping thread under needle. Continue for length of stitch, keeping needle vertical.

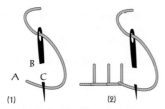

## Centering the Design

Fold the fabric in half horizontally, then vertically. Place a pin in the fold point to mark the center. Locate the center of the design on the graph. Begin stitching all designs at the center point of graph and fabric.

## Cleaning Completed Work

When stitching is complete, soak fabric in cold water with a mild soap for five to 10 minutes. Rinse well and roll in a towel to remove excess water. Do not wring. Place work face down on a dry towel and iron on warm setting until the fabric is dry

## Cord Piping

Center cording on wrong side of the bias strip and fold fabric over it, aligning raw edges. Using zipper foot, machine-stitch through both layers of fabric close to cording. Trim seam allowance to ¼".

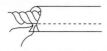

## Couched Straight Stitch

See chart keys for stitch information on floss or thread color, number of strands, and placement.
Complete a straight stitch. Make certain floss or thread is flat. See (1).

Make short tight straight stitches across base to "couch" the straight stitch. Come up on one side of the floss. Go down on the opposite side of the floss. See (2).

Tack at varying intervals. Completed Couched Straight Stitch. See (3).

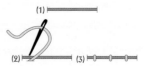

## Cross-stitch

Stitches are done in a row or, if necessary, one at a time in an area. Stitching is done by coming up through a hole between woven threads at A. Then, go down at B, the hole diagonally across from A. Come back up at C and down at D, etc. See (1).

Complete the top stitches to create an "X". All top stitches should lie in the same direction. Come up at E and go down at F, come up at G and go down at H, etc. See (2).

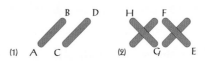

## Cross-stitch, Half

The stitch actually fits three-fourths of the area. Make the longer stitch in direction of the slanted line on the graph. Bring needle and thread up at A, down at B, up at C, and down at D.

## Fabrics & Waste Canvas

Cross-stitch is usually worked on even-weave fabrics specifically manufactured for counted thread needlework. These fabrics are woven with the same number of vertical and horizontal threads per inch.

Because the number of threads in the fabric is equal in each direction, each stitch will be the same size. The number of threads per inch in even-weave fabrics determines the size of a finished design.

Waste canvas is a coarse, fabric-like substance used as a guide for cross-stitching on fabrics other than even-weaves. Cut the waste canvas 1" larger on all sides than the finished design size. Baste it to the fabric to be stitched. Complete the stitching. Then, dampen the stitched area with cold water. Pull the waste canvas threads out one at a time with tweezers. It is easier to pull all the threads running in one direction first; then pull out the opposite threads. Allow the stitching to dry. Place face down on a towel and iron.

# Floss & Carrying Floss

Six-strand embroidery floss is normally used for cross-stitch. For each graphed design there is a color code. All numbers and color names on this code represent DMC brands of floss. The number of strands used for cross-stitching is determined by the thread count of the fabric. See project instructions for suggested strand amounts.

Use 18" lengths of floss. For best coverage, separate strands. Dampen with wet sponge. Then put together number of strands required for fabric used.

To carry floss, weave floss under the previously worked stitches on the back. Do not carry thread across any fabric that is not or will not be stitched. Loose threads, especially dark ones, will show through the fabric.

# French Knot

Bring needle up at A, using two strands of embroidery floss. Loosely wrap floss once around needle. See (1).

Place needle at B, next to A. Pull floss taut and push needle down through fabric. See (2). Carry floss across back of work between knots.

Completed French Knot. See (3).

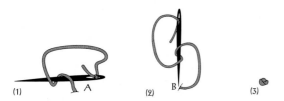

(1)  A  (2)  B  (3)

# Lazy Daisy

Bring the needle up at A. Keep the thread flat, untwisted, and full. Put the needle down through fabric at B and up through at C, keeping the thread under the needle to form a loop. Pull the thread through, leaving the loop loose and full. To hold the loop in place, go down on other side of thread near C, forming a straight stitch over loop. See (1).

Completed Lazy Daisy. See (2).

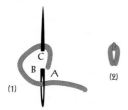

C
B  A
(1)  (2)

# Marking on Fabric

Always use a dressmaker's pen or chalk to mark on fabric. It will wash out when piece is finished.

# Needles

Use a #24 or #26 tapestry needle for all designs in this book.

Never leave needle in design area of fabric. It may leave rust or a permanent impression on fabric.

# Patterns

Use tracing paper to trace patterns. Be sure to transfer all information.

# Preparing Fabric

Cut fabric at least 3" larger on all sides than finished design size to ensure enough space for desired assembly. If the design is used to embellish a project that will be finished further, check instructions for specific fabric allowances. A 3" margin is the minimum amount of space that allows for comfortably finishing the edges of the design.

To prevent fraying, machine-zigzag or hand-stitch along raw edges of the fabric, or apply liquid fray preventer.

# Securing the Floss

Insert needle up from the underside of the fabric at starting point. Hold 1" of thread behind the fabric and stitch over it, securing with the first few stitches. To finish thread, run under four or more stitches on the back of the design. Never knot floss, unless working on clothing.

Another method of securing floss is the waste knot. Knot floss and insert needle from the right side of the fabric about 1" from design area. Work several stitches over the thread to secure. Cut off the knot later.

# Slip-stitch

Insert needle at A, taking a small stitch and slide it through the folded edge of fabric about ⅛" to ¼", bring needle out at B.

A
B

# Smyrna Cross

Work a cross-stitch. Work an upright cross-stitch on top. They may be done in a different color.

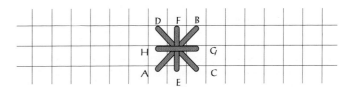

D  F  B
H    G
A    C
E

# Smyrna Cross, Elongated

Work a cross-stitch. Work an upright cross-stitch, making E elongated. They may be done in a different color.

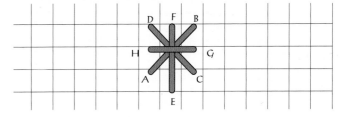

D  F  B
H    G
A    C
E

# Metric Equivalency

mm-millimetres    cm-centimetres

inches to millimetres and centimetres

| inches | mm | cm | inches | cm | inches | cm |
|--------|-----|------|--------|------|--------|-------|
| ⅛ | 3 | 0.3 | 9 | 22.9 | 30 | 76.2 |
| ¼ | 6 | 0.6 | 10 | 25.4 | 31 | 78.7 |
| ½ | 13 | 1.3 | 12 | 30.5 | 33 | 83.8 |
| ⅝ | 16 | 1.6 | 13 | 33.0 | 34 | 86.4 |
| ¾ | 19 | 1.9 | 14 | 35.6 | 35 | 88.9 |
| ⅞ | 22 | 2.2 | 15 | 38.1 | 36 | 91.4 |
| 1 | 25 | 2.5 | 16 | 40.6 | 37 | 94.0 |
| 1¼ | 32 | 3.2 | 17 | 43.2 | 38 | 96.5 |
| 1½ | 38 | 3.8 | 18 | 45.7 | 39 | 99.1 |
| 1¾ | 44 | 4.4 | 19 | 48.3 | 40 | 101.6 |
| 2 | 51 | 5.1 | 20 | 50.8 | 41 | 104.1 |
| 2½ | 64 | 6.4 | 21 | 53.3 | 42 | 106.7 |
| 3 | 76 | 7.6 | 22 | 55.9 | 43 | 109.2 |
| 3½ | 89 | 8.9 | 23 | 58.4 | 44 | 111.8 |
| 4 | 102 | 10.2 | 24 | 61.0 | 45 | 114.3 |
| 4½ | 114 | 11.4 | 25 | 63.5 | 46 | 116.8 |
| 5 | 127 | 12.7 | 26 | 66.0 | 47 | 119.4 |
| 6 | 152 | 15.2 | 27 | 68.6 | 48 | 121.9 |
| 7 | 178 | 17.8 | 28 | 71.1 | 49 | 124.5 |
| 8 | 203 | 20.3 | 29 | 73.7 | 50 | 127.0 |

# Index